Effective
Feedback Skills

Effective Feedback Skills

second edition

TIM RUSSELL

KOGAN
PAGE

**For Edward and Alexandra,
without whom this book would have been
written in half the time**

First published in 1994
Second edition 1998

Kogan Page Limited
120 Pentonville Road
London N1 9JN

© Tim Russell, 1994

British Library Cataloguing in Publication Data

A CIP record of this book is available from the British Library.

ISBN 0 7494 2569 5

Typeset by Koinonia Ltd, Bury
Printed and bound in Great Britain by
Biddles Ltd, Guildford and King's Lynn

Contents

Series Editor's Foreword

Organizations get things done when people do their jobs effectively. To make this happen they need to be well trained. A number of people are likely to be involved in this training by identifying the needs of the organization and of the individual, by selecting or designing appropriate training to meet these needs, by delivering it and assessing how effective it was. It is not only 'professional' or full-time trainers who are involved in this process; personnel managers, line managers, supervisors and job holders are all likely to have a part to play.

This series has been written for all those who get involved with training in some way or another, whether they are senior personnel managers trying to link the goals of the organization with training needs or job holders who have been given responsibility for training newcomers. Therefore, the series is essentially a practical one which focuses on specific aspects of the training function. This is not to say that the theoretical underpinnings of the practical aspects of training are unimportant. Anyone seriously interested in training is strongly encouraged to look beyond 'what to do' and 'how to do it' and to delve into the areas of why things are done in a particular way. The series has become so popular that it is intended to include additional volumes whenever a need is found for practical guidelines in some area of training.

The authors have been selected because they have considerable practical experience. All have shared, at some time, the same difficulties, frustrations and satisfactions of being involved in training and are now in a position to share with others some helpful and practical guidelines.

In this book, Tim Russell shows us the importance of feedback in the process of learning and provides sound guidelines on how it should be given. The problems of giving and receiving feedback are similar to those encountered during appraisal. It is a process which can cause difficulty, if not embarrassment, for both parties, something which they may both want to get over quickly. As a result, it can become superficial. When this happens a learning opportunity is lost.

All trainers like to believe that they are giving of their best but unless they master the skills of giving feedback, they will be less than effective. The amount and nature of feedback that individuals can take and act upon depends on their previous experience of feedback and their capacity for receiving feedback. Trainers need to be able to gauge an individual's capacity and to cater to it in such a way that those whom they train look forward to such sessions as a positive opportunity for development.

Tim Russell explains an interesting difference between feedback and debriefing. It is a useful way to focus upon the skills needed by the trainer, the structure of a feedback and debrief session and the ways in which the trainee's capacity for feedback can be gauged.

This book is valuable for anyone who has responsibility for training and development – and there are many line managers who would find it of benefit in dealing with those day-to-day aspects of staff performance which need to be corrected, developed or recognized.

ROGER BUCKLEY

Introduction

Occasionally, participants on my training workshops confess to me during the programme that they have not slept the night before they were due to attend. Their experience from previous training had been so horrendous that they had tried all sorts of measures to avoid attending this one – perhaps even getting their mother to write a sick note! The reason, they often explain, was insensitive feedback from the trainer. They were embarrassed in front of their peers, ridiculed in a role play or humiliated on video.

While some instructors might terrify their learners, others can be so nervous about upsetting their trainees, that they skirt around issues and leave people totally confused, not knowing if they have learned anything at all.

Probably the single most important skill for any trainer is being able to give feedback to trainees on their performance. Unless trainees can find out what they are doing right, they will not know to do it again. Unless they can find out what they are doing wrong, they will see no need to change. Unless they are shown the correct way to operate, they will not know how to change. Feedback skills are necessary for all trainers in all areas, from part-time to full-time, from craft instructor to management tutor.

Ironically, though, feedback is one of the most complex areas for trainers to master. The reason for giving feedback has to be thoroughly analysed to determine for whose benefit it is to be done. The appropriate climate has to be set and the methods and styles of feedback decided. If we give too little feedback, the trainee's rate of learning is slowed down and training time will increase. If we give too much of the wrong sort of feedback, we can sour the relationship between trainee and trainer, if not the whole concept of training, for life.

Feedback after a group exercise is quite different from feedback during a one-to-one coaching session, though just as important. Video cameras and recording machines mean that we can show the learners exactly what they did, but seeing the situation may not make it any more palatable for them to talk about it and the presence of the equipment might have inhibited their performance. Observers will have an impact, as will the thought that the results of the training might be sent back to a manager.

The terms 'feedback' and 'debriefing' are commonly used in all aspects of training and teaching, yet they have different meanings to different people. Frequently the words are used interchangeably and the definitions vary according to the circumstances. For the purpose of this book, I have defined the words in particular ways to highlight the different functions that they serve. These definitions are used consistently and since drawing the distinction, I have radically changed the way that I review trainees' performances with a significant improvement in results.

This book is divided into four parts. The first part discusses the issues and terms involved in feedback and differentiates between four types of learning. It describes briefly how people learn and leads to a crucial distinction between 'feedback' and 'debriefing'. As defined in the book, 'feedback' is the process of comparing a trainee's performance with the required standard for the learning. It then reinforces what was done correctly and plans improvements for what was not done properly. 'Feedback' is used in areas of training where there is a right and a wrong, where there is an objective standard which the learner has or has not achieved.

'Debriefing' is used in the other areas of training where there is *no* right or wrong. In these forms of learning, the trainer's role is to allow the learners to consider the advantages, disadvantages and possible reactions to several alternatives. There is never a guaranteed outcome and the purpose of 'debriefing' is to explore options rather than confirm any particular course of action. Debriefing is linked to the concept of 'judgement', a category that I have added to the traditional taxonomy of knowledge, skills and attitude with excellent benefits.

Part II of the book discusses 'feedback'. After setting the contexts for giving feedback, we look at how and when to give it and then how trainees receive it. We look at how to judge when the trainee has had enough and what to do then.

In Part III we review 'debriefing'. After again setting the contexts, we look at styles of debriefing and how to handle the various trainees who will be involved in the debrief session.

Finally, in Part IV, we consider another vital aspect of feedback and debriefing: reporting back. The whole question of reporting trainee performance back to managers has created enormous controversy over the years and in this part we look at the various arguments and suggest how reports should be made.

Although the primary setting of this book is in the world of industry and commerce, it will also be very applicable to lecturers and teachers in higher and further education, particularly as the relationship between industry and education is becoming much closer.

As the approaches used to feedback are a little radical and some of the definitions may differ slightly from conventional usage, it is recommended that the reader establishes the frameworks of the book by reading Part I first and then moves to which other sections meet the most immediate needs.

The material for the book is drawn from my own experiences of being a trainer for many years and a learner for many more. As a trainer of trainers, I have the advantage of simultaneously implementing what I am teaching and learning more at the same time. I would like to thank the hundreds of participants from my courses who have helped me to learn about feedback and I apologise to them if, occasionally, I still get it a little wrong!

I should also like to thank my wife, Elizabeth, for her advice, support and feedback.

I
The Issues
and the
Terms

1 What People Can Learn and How They Learn

▷   SUMMARY   ◁

This chapter:
- classifies what people can learn into four component parts;
- identifies the key attribute of each component;
- describes a model of how people learn;
- presents a matrix showing the purpose of different training techniques;
- considers the effect of different learning styles.

In determining whether we are to give feedback or a debrief, it is important to be able to distinguish between the different types of learning that exist. Such a classification also helps in the design of the training session and the selection of the appropriate training technique. If the wrong technique is chosen there can be enormous confusion between trainer and trainees about the purpose of the training and the relevance of the feedback.

The Classification

There are several ways of classifying what people can learn, but one of the simplest divides everything that can be learned into one, or a combination, of: knowledge, skills and attitudes. This is one of the most popular taxonomies and has been used for many years. However, it seems to miss an important aspect of learning, so it is suggested that a fourth category, judgement, as described below, is included.

Knowledge

Knowledge includes those areas that we learn where *there is a right or a wrong answer*. It includes facts, policies, information and procedures. Hopefully, trainers in knowledge have the right information and it is their job to transmit this to the trainees so that they too possess those facts. If the learner disagrees with the trainer in the knowledge area, then, by definition, the learner is wrong – or the trainer should be looking for a new job! It is as absolute as that. The trainees might not like the procedures, but the fact is that that is the way they are. With knowledge, the trainees either know the information or they do not. It is not possible to 'half know' something, though it is, of course, possible to know half of it. A learner driver has to learn to be able to recognize the traffic signs of the Highway Code. The triangle with two children warns of a school, not a hospital or low bridge. The learner either knows that or they do not. With more exposure and repetition, they will be able to recognize more signs.

Skills

Skills are practical abilities to do something, where *trainees improve with practice*. There are three types of skill:

- physical – that which is done with the body, for example, typing and operating machinery;
- mental – that which is done with the mind, for example, calculations and clerical work;
- social – dealing with people, for example, interviewing and running meetings.

Because skills develop with practice, the concept of 'degrees of skill' becomes significant. It is not appropriate to divide people simply into skilled and unskilled. It is the *level* of their skill that is important and training designers should specify the desired level of competence so that they know when to stop training. For a trainee who will only be using a skill occasionally, a fairly basic level of skill might be sufficient and it would be unnecessary, as well as expensive and time-consuming, to train to a higher level. The level of skill required would clearly have a bearing on the intensity of the feedback given.

Judgement

Judgement is an addition to the familiar classification, but an important one, particularly within the context of feedback and debriefing. The definition of judgement used throughout this book is the ability to solve problems where *there is no provably right or wrong answer* at the time that the decision is made. (This makes judgement fundamentally different from knowledge where there *is* a right or a wrong answer.) With hindsight anyone can say whether the judgement turned out to be successful or not, but at that time there could be no such assurance. Further, the implementation of any solution will change the nature of the problem. Most problem solving and decision making about people is judgement. It involves taking a unique situation, weighing up the factors that are likely to affect that situation, using experience, initiative and intuition and then making a decision. Because every case in judgement is different from the one before, and the one after, there is little point in concentrating on the decision itself. By the time that the decision has been made the nature of the problem has changed and that problem will never appear in that exact same form again. As each case is unique and different, the handling of it cannot be a skill, as skill is an activity where the trainee improves with practice. With judgement there is never the opportunity to have a second attempt. It is more useful, therefore, to consider the ingredients of the case and how they might interact so that this can be stored in the trainees' memories for when they meet a related, but still unique, situation.

A simple example of judgement might be training supervisors how to deal with staff who are late for work. If there is a clocking-in system or the company operates flexible working hours, there is no judgement that the supervisor needs to make. He or she would merely need the *knowledge* that such systems exist and any transgressions would be dealt with by the personnel department. If supervisors did have to deal with late comers themselves, they would need to *know* the company policies, procedures and values and then, within that framework, make a decision. Each late-comer would be dealt with as an individual case, after the supervisor has weighed all the appropriate factors. These factors might include:

- how late the person was;
- whether they had said that they might be late;
- how long they had worked with the company;
- whether it was known that they had personal problems;
- what their work record was like;
- etc, etc.

One very relevant factor would be how many times the person had been late before. If this was the very first time, some supervisors would recommend that nothing be said – and they would not be wrong because they have the discretion to make such a decision and it does not break any rules. Other supervisors might suggest that they do approach the individual on the first occasion of lateness so that it does not become custom and practice – and they would not be wrong either. However, the trainee supervisor who says that the person should be fired is wrong. Their idea is factually against the company policy and against employment legislation. They are not wrong in their judgement, though: they are wrong in their knowledge.

Another possible decision might be to allow the individual to come to explain why they are late. This also is not wrong, but it might demand that the supervisor makes additional judgements on how long to wait for the explanation before they assume that there will not be one and then what to do. In this case, the offender has now made two mistakes: the first was in being late and the second was in not coming to explain why. Certainly, the late-comer committed the first error, but the supervisor allowed the second one to occur by waiting. Had the supervisor approached the staff member at the moment that they arrived for work, the second mistake would not have happened. With judgement, you only have one attempt at making the decision and when that decision has been implemented the nature of the problem has changed, as time has moved on. Of course, doing nothing is also implementing a decision, albeit rather passively.

Judgement, as defined here, is therefore different from knowledge, as there is not a right or wrong answer; different from skill, as the trainee cannot practise it; and different from attitude because it is observable. Learning knowledge, skills and attitudes will help to develop judgement, in the same way that increased knowledge will help with skills, though they are not in themselves sufficient. Judgement is a separate learning activity and is essential for anyone who has to make decisions.

The judgement always takes place in the brain as the trainees think and then decide. Actually addressing the late staff member and implementing the decision is a social skill as here there is an interaction with another person. Clearly there is a difference between the intellectual process of deciding and the interactive process of implementing and it is certainly possible that a trainee who is good at one may not be good at the other.

Attitudes

Attitudes are the *collection of beliefs, values and prejudices which determine the way people behave*. They are not always based on sound foundations and frequently the source of the attitude cannot be traced. As attitudes are so intangible and non-specific, some trainers prefer to assume that they do not exist and concentrate only on trying to help people to learn new, observable behaviours. More attitudinally-based trainers, however, claim that as attitudes are the roots of people's behaviour, it is worth the time and effort to work on the underlying attitude rather than on a host of individual behaviours.

The Combinations

In reality little learning is purely knowledge, skills, judgement or attitude alone, but is a combination of the above and involves aspects of all four components. For example, learning to ride a bicycle might involve, among many other things:

- knowledge   – the functions of the various parts of the bicycle
  - the Highway Code
- physical skills   – balance
  - steering
  - pedalling
  - operating the brakes and gears
- mental skills   – measuring stopping distances
  - assessing the space between vehicles
- judgement   – deciding when to accelerate and when to slow down
  - deciding which gear to use
- attitudes   – the importance of courtesy to other road users
  - the potential dangers of the bicycle.

How People Learn

How people learn is an immensely complex subject and researchers are breaking new ground constantly. The parallels between human intelligence and artificial intelligence have led to the development of models of learning which cast light on the human processes. A particularly helpful approach to describe the function of feedback and debriefing is the 'input – process – output' model.

The 'Input – Process – Output' Model

For training to be complete, the trainees must go through the following steps:

- *input* so that they have access to the new information to be learned. This is where they are presented with the new knowledge, skills, judgement or attitude;

- *process* so that they can consolidate this information and fix it in their minds. The real learning takes place here, as the learners assimilate the lesson and link it to other previous learning;
- *output* so that they can demonstrate the newly acquired learning both to the trainer, who can see that learning has taken place, and to themselves, so that they will raise their own confidence.

Additionally, learners need to have information about their performance so that they can correct and improve it, where necessary. This might be achieved either by going through the 'input' again in, perhaps, a different way or by finding a more effective means of 'processing' it. This can be seen diagrammatically, in Figure 1.1 as:

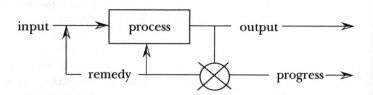

Figure 1.1 *The 'input – process – output' model of learning*

The new learning is introduced through the 'input', is consolidated by the 'process' and demonstrated by the 'output'.

The 'input' is where the learner is exposed to the new knowledge, skills, judgement or attitude. The trainer will be able to plan what this 'input' will be and will be able to ensure that the learner is presented with the correct information in the most appropriate way. Breaking down the 'input' into digestible chunks and adding visual aids and humour, together with all the other good practices of training will help the 'input' to go in.

Despite all the best efforts of the instructor, however, it is the 'process' stage where the real learning occurs, where the true consolidation takes place. The trainer will initiate the 'process' stage with an exercise but cannot see or hear what is actually going on in the learner's mind. Because the 'process' can never be seen it is positioned inside a box in the model. A thorough 'input' and well planned 'processing' should help the message to be learned in the appropriate way, but for true confirmation of what has actually been taken in, the learner must give an 'output'.

It is only when the learner produces an answer or a demonstration that their level of learning can be assessed. Their 'output' is then compared with the right answer or the required standard (represented by the symbol ⊗) and progress is confirmed or remedies devised. If it is found that the learners' 'output' does not meet the required standard, it is either that they misunderstood the 'input' or they 'processed' the 'input' incorrectly. The tutor will, therefore, go through the 'input' or the 'process' stages again. Clearly, the skilled trainer will find different ways to present the 'input' and different methods of 'processing'. If the trainees did not succeed with the first form of training, they probably will not do much better if it is simply repeated.

If any one of the three stages of 'input', 'process' or 'output' is missing, then the learning breaks down. If there is no 'input', there is nothing to 'process'. If there is no 'processing', there can be no 'output' and with no 'output' there is no progress.

Certainly, as can be seen from Figure 1.1, the trainees' 'output' will become part of their subsequent 'input' and so they will learn from both their successes and their failures. It is preferable to begin the cycle at the 'input' stage so that the learners know what it is that they are trying to 'process'. There is then a greater likelihood of a successful 'output'. The training technique known as the 'discovery method' begins the model at the 'process' stage. The trainees are set an exercise from which they generate 'outputs'. These are then assessed and become the 'input' for further 'processing'. Clearly, this approach to training must be carefully planned. Without the 'input', there is a much higher chance that the 'process' could produce 'outputs' that are wrong rather than right. The feedback to the trainees could thus be more slanted towards failures than successes, leading to the demoralization discussed in Chapter 5.

The Training Techniques Matrix

Putting together what people can learn – knowledge, skills, judgement and attitudes – with how they learn – 'input', 'process' and 'output' – a matrix of training techniques can be drawn up as shown in Figure 1.2. The correct selection of training technique is essential for the appropriate use of feedback and debriefing.

By selecting one technique from each column, trainers can devise lessons that cover all three components of learning. For example, knowledge sessions could be conducted by: lecture/questions/answers, or a video/exercise/report back, etc.

The decision about which technique to use will be made after considering a number of factors including the number of trainees, their geographical dispersion, the frequency at which the sessions are going to be run and the learning styles of the students.

	INPUT	PROCESS	OUTPUT
KNOWLEDGE	lecture reading explanation video/audio	questions discussions exercises	answers reports back
SKILLS	demonstration	practice*	performance
JUDGEMENT	trainee experience case studies exercises/games	discussions debriefing	reports back
ATTITUDES	videos prestige speakers role reversal self-awareness instruments	group discussion	performance

Figure 1.2 *The Training Techniques Matrix*

*It is worth noting that for social skills the form of practice used to process the demonstration is often referred to as a 'role play'. However, as explained later, this is not always a helpful label.

Learning Styles

Trainees' learning styles will affect the form of feedback that they prefer and from which they learn best. Various models have been developed to describe the different learning styles that are apparent in trainees. For the sake of brevity, only one will be described here. A popular approach, put forward by Peter Honey and Alan Mumford (1983), distinguishes between four styles: the Activist, the Reflector, the Theorist and the Pragmatist. While we probably all learn through all four styles, we appear to have one or two preferences and perhaps one or two that we are not so good at. Ideally, we should try to develop all four channels and so improve our rate of learning, but for the trainees on our programmes it is likely that will bring a range of styles.

The *Activists* are the people whose preferred method of learning is through being involved. They like exercises and practice and are less keen on sitting still. Their preferred form of feedback is likely to be short, sharp and snappy with plenty of opportunity to try things out again.

The *Reflectors* are the more thoughtful characters. They are usually quieter than the other styles and would like time to think and ponder over the feedback they are receiving and the observations they are making about other people. They are usually less keen to be the first at practice sessions and will need a period of reflection before wanting a second attempt to rectify a criticized point.

The *Theorists* feel a need to have a theory, a model or an underpinning explanation for the feedback. Their favourite word is probably, 'Why?', which is intended so that they can gain a greater understanding of the subject. It is not usually a challenge to the instructor on the feedback they are receiving.

The *Pragmatist* is less concerned with the reasons and more interested in the action. Their favourite questions are probably, 'What?' and 'How?'. The theory is less important than knowing what they actually have to do or say to make the skill better. Their preferred feedback is specific and directly applicable.

Review

In this chapter we have considered what and how people learn. These distinctions are crucial in the understanding of the purpose of feedback and its difference from debriefing. In the design of training sessions, it is important that the correct distinction is made between 'knowledge', 'skills', 'judgement' and 'attitude' and that the appropriate choice of training technique is then made and fitted to the learning styles of the learners. The importance of the concept of judgement cannot be over-emphasized. With this ground work done we can move directly into defining and distinguishing feedback from debriefing.

CHECKLIST FOR THE TRAINER

- Does your training design include objectives with measurable desired standards of performance?
- Does your design show clear distinctions between knowledge, skills, judgement and attitudes, particularly judgement?
- Do these have levels of competence specified?
- Do the training techniques conform to the Training Techniques Matrix?
- Does every session have an 'input', a 'process' and an 'output'?
- Are the training techniques taking account of the learning styles of the learners?

---

2 Feedback and Debriefing

▷   **SUMMARY**   ◁

This chapter:
- defines 'feedback';
- defines 'debriefing';
- explains the importance of distinguishing these.

The terms 'feedback' and 'debriefing', as used in this book, have distinctly different meanings and an appreciation of this distinction is crucial for maximizing the return on the investment of time and money in learners doing practical work. Where the word 'review' is used this refers to the whole discussion of a trainee's practice and may well include feedback on the knowledge and skills and debrief on the judgements.

What is Feedback?

All good training sessions have objectives written for those sessions and those objectives have desired standards of performance. For knowledge, this might be that the trainees can demonstrate they have certain information. For example:

> The trainees will be able to name all 13 founding states of America, from memory, within five minutes.

For skills it might be that they can demonstrate a certain level of competence in that skill. For example:

> The trainee will be able to juggle three oranges for two minutes without dropping any of them.

If the teaching session does not have a definable, measurable outcome, the trainer will not know which students need more help nor when to stop training them. If trainees do not meet the standards they will be unable to perform their job to the required standard. If they are trained beyond the desired standard, time and money has been spent unnecessarily. Mager (1991) describes these essentials of training excellently.

Feedback is defined here as letting trainees know what they have done that has reached the standard, so that they can reproduce that behaviour, and what they have done that has not reached the standard, so that plans can be agreed with them on how to prevent a recurrence of that behaviour and how to progress towards the required standard. Achieving the standard is obviously correct behaviour and therefore 'right'. Not achieving it is incorrect behaviour and therefore 'wrong'. The concepts of right and wrong are not in any way criticisms of the learners themselves but are factual descriptions of whether or not their performance has reached the required standard. Clearly this is a crucial trainer skill. If trainees do not know what they are doing right or wrong, they will not see a need to change. If plans for improvement are not made they will not know how to change. Only through feedback can development be achieved, or, according to the 'input-process-output' model, only with feedback can progress be made.

Implicit within the definition, however, is the concept of measurable standards. If the trainees are to be told what they have done right or wrong, there must be a right or a wrong in what they have done. Applying the classification from the first chapter, we can see that feedback is applicable in areas of knowledge where, by definition, there is a right and a wrong answer. It is also applicable in skills training. Once we have been able to specify the level of skill that we want the trainees to achieve, it is then relatively easy to ascertain whether or not they have achieved that level of competence. If the desired typing speed is set at 40 words per minute, we can count the number of words and set a watch. However, if the speed is only set as 'reasonably fast', there will be a wide variation of interpretations.

Attitude training will always present a problem. Attitudes are internal to individuals and it is only by their outward behaviour that we can gain a clue as to what their real attitudes might be. Whether their behaviour is right or wrong can be assessed, though whether this behaviour is indicative of their true attitude will always be questionable. The bright trainees will know what they are supposed to do or say, because the trainers will have been labouring the points for hours if not days. They may well conform to these behaviours in the learning environment just to keep the trainers happy, but have no intention of maintaining this after the teaching periods.

But it is with judgement training that the real problems of feedback arise. With judgement, by definition, there is no right or wrong answer, yet for feedback, as defined here, there has to be a right or wrong standard. Clearly, therefore, it is not legitimate to give feedback on judgements at the time that those judgements are made. We can certainly review those judgements in the light of our, and other people's, experiences and, with the benefit of hindsight, discuss what the outcome was. If we were to give *feedback* on someone's decision it could only be on knowledge involved in making that decision. We could tell a trainee that their idea was unacceptable if it was against company policy, rules and procedures or was against a legal or ethical code. This feedback would be on knowledge, however, as they would be wrong. The trainer should not criticize any idea that was within the rules, even though it would not be what the trainer would do themselves. The idea might be perfect for that particular learner even though the trainer might find it personally offensive.

In the previous chapter we considered the simple decision of dealing with a member of staff who is late for work. One trainee's suggestion might be to stand in front of the late-comer, look at their watch and make a sarcastic quip. This would not be wrong, even though it might be something the trainer would never do themselves. It does not break any rules or codes and is therefore acceptable. The trainer who says otherwise is in danger of imposing his or her personal value system on the trainee. The trainee could become confused as the trainer could not support the criticism with facts. Later, when a different instructor says that it is acceptable to be sarcastic, the credibility of the training department will be questioned. Of course, the first trainer can point out the potential hazards of sarcasm with some people some times, but they should not tell the trainee that they are actually wrong.

Having decided to be sarcastic, the trainee must obviously have the social skills of being able to pull it off. If the attempted sarcasm contains any sexual or racial slurs, the trainee is now wrong as they have broken the knowledge of the rules.

It is, perhaps, worth restating the definition of judgement as being the ability to solve problems where there is no provably right or wrong answer at the time that the decision is made.

What is Debriefing?

Debriefing is the process of reviewing the trainees' judgements and considering the relative merits of their decision with those of alternatives.

It is not that their decision is wrong, because with judgement there is no wrong decision, except where the knowledge is wrong. The purpose of debriefing is to broaden people's thinking and increase their options to act. They can then learn from the experiences of others without necessarily having had that direct experience themselves.

EXAMPLE 1

As Chris, a learner driver, is approaching traffic lights they turn to amber. He has the choice of stopping or of continuing. Under the circumstances at the time either action would be equally acceptable. After the lesson, Pat, his instructor, debriefs him on his decision by discussing those factors that would be taken into consideration when deciding how to handle future amber lights. These factors might include traffic and weather conditions, speed and distances. Chris was not wrong in his decision. Pat's debrief will help to prepare him for future sets of traffic lights that he will meet in his driving career.

EXAMPLE 2

Having listened to the customer's needs and presented the product's features and benefits, Harriet decided to go for the close of the sales interview to try to gain a commitment from the customer to buy. The customer did not buy the product, but at the time that she made her move, no one could have predicted exactly how the customer would react. Back in the car, Sarah, her sales manager, debriefed the situation by reviewing what processes she went through and what options were available for tackling future customers. At the same time, Sarah probably felt that she too gained from the debriefing by broadening her experience. In the approach she did use, she conformed exactly to the procedures that she had been taught during training.

In some cases, managers and companies feel uneasy allowing the junior staff to make these independent decisions and to use their discretion. In these cases they often produce guidelines, or even policies, for the staff to follow, reducing the judgements to knowledge. What would be debriefing of the judgement thus becomes feedback on whether or not they knew the policy.

The Importance of the Distinction between Feedback and Debriefing

To operate effectively in most areas, people have to learn, first, how to make decisions and second, how to implement them. In training terms, these are judgements and then skills.

When discussing with trainees *what* they have decided, we can certainly point out the advantages and disadvantages and alternative solutions, but we cannot label one answer as right and the others wrong. However, when we look at *how* the decision was implemented, we can criticize and give feedback because the trainee would have been successful or would have failed.

At the next set of traffic lights, green turned to amber again, just as Chris approached. This time he decided to stop, slammed on the brakes, screeched, skidded and stalled the car. His judgement to stop could have been perfectly sound, but his physical skill at stopping the car would receive some feedback from Pat on how to stop the car in 80 metres from 30 mph in dry conditions without skidding, screeching or stalling.

As Harriet went to close the sale, she looked at the floor, fidgeted and mumbled. Her timing might have been fine, but she is lacking in the social skills of closing the sale. Sarah set up a role play with Harriet as the customer and herself as the sales representative and demonstrated the skills of closing.

As much training involves decisions and implementation, the review of performance will involve both debriefing and feedback. This review could be at the end of the practical session or during it, according to the circumstances, as we shall discuss later in this book.

For trainers, the distinction between judgement/debriefing and skills/feedback is important. If the trainer is not clear, the trainees will not know if they thought of a reasonable idea and implemented it badly, a poor decision and implemented it well, or a poorer decision and implemented it worse!

Chris and Harriet will both know that they were not successful at what they were trying to achieve, but it is up to Pat and Sarah to help them distinguish between their decision and their inability to implement it.

Review

We have seen in this chapter the importance of distinguishing feedback from debriefing. Feedback will be on the knowledge and skills; debriefing will be on the judgement.

CHECKLIST FOR THE TRAINER

- Do your training sessions distinguish clearly those areas for debriefing from those areas for feedback?
- What is the purpose of your training exercises and games?
- Do they train in judgement or skills? Are they followed by debriefing or feedback?
- What is the purpose of your role plays? Do they train in judgement or skills? Are they followed by debriefing or feedback?

II
Feedback

3 The Contexts for Feedback

▷ SUMMARY ◁

This chapter considers the contexts for giving feedback:
- on the job;
- off the job;
- after knowledge and skills sessions;
- after judgement and attitude sessions;
- the role play.

Feedback is an essential skill for learning knowledge and skills and there are many different circumstances when feedback will be given within a training and teaching context.

On the Job

Some of the very best training takes place on the job. The equipment is real, the environment similar to real life and the output of the skill has meaning. The trainees can see the relevance and the application of the learning and their attention will be high. However, as the reality of the training increases so too do the risks. The consequences of a mistake will be potentially more dangerous or expensive. Making frequent mistakes will dent the trainees' confidence more in an on-the-job situation than in an off-the-job experience. To counter this most on-the-job training is conducted with one or a very small number of trainees. The role of the on-the-job instructor and their relationship with the trainee will usually be different from the off-the-job counterpart. The on-the-job trainer will often be part-time at that function, spending the bulk of their working time as a skilled practitioner. This can mean that they are also the trainees' supervisor or immediate manager who subsequently might be appraising them on job performance as well. There are clearly both benefits and disadvantages to this. The on-the-job coach will be able to provide continual guidance and coaching for the trainees' whole learning within that department. However, the trainees are more likely to feel threatened when it is their actual manager training them.

The basis on which on-the-job instructors are selected is not to be taken lightly. The coach must be an excellent exponent of the skills to be taught otherwise they can only teach bad practices. They must also model the attitudes that the company wants to encourage.

> After a half-day induction into the bus company, Jim was introduced to Peter who was to be his on-the-job instructor. Peter had been a bus conductor for five years and, as he 'knew the ropes' was appointed to the training position and the extra bonus that it held. By the end of his first week at the job, Jim knew all the routes around town and all the operating and safety procedures. He also knew how to collect fares without issuing tickets, how to minimize the actual number of passengers boarding a bus and how, in connivance with his driver, to fake a breakdown at the furthest distance from the bus depot just before the end of their shift. A coded telephone message to the rescue mechanics would ensure that help was a long time coming so that the overtime earned could be maximized.

Some excellent technicians are not necessarily also capable instructors and it usually well worth the investment to train these part-time instructors in instructional techniques.

Off the Job

Off-the-job instruction is usually more formal in its presentation, there are more trainees and more structure. The trainers are more likely to be full-time presenters of the material and their level of expertise of training might be higher. Because there is a more defined timetable, there is less flexibility and less opportunity for the trainers to allow the participants to experiment and practise as much as both parties would like. Practical sessions are more likely to be simulations leading to a slightly unreal feel to the whole process. This has the advantage that there will be few risks of anything dire going wrong, though the commitment of the participants to practise can sometimes be reduced.

After Knowledge and Skills Sessions

Feedback is based on the output of the trainee's process and the methods of processing are similar to those used for testing. It is the purpose, rather than the mechanism, that is different. In Chapter 9 we look at the measurement and testing aspects in more detail.

After Knowledge Sessions

By definition, with knowledge there is a right and a wrong, so it is legitimate and very helpful for learners to be informed what they have done right, what they have done wrong and what the right answer is. Knowing something in theory, though, does not necessarily mean that the individual can put it into practice. From the 'Training Techniques Matrix' in Chapter 1, we saw that the output of the learning will be answers from questions or quizzes and reports back from discussions (where the learners have been discussing facts rather than judgements). Feedback on the accuracy of the output facts can be made by simple comparison with the input from the trainer or from the reading, video or audio material.

After Skills Sessions

When learning skills there are two aspects that trainers should consider for feedback – the *product* of the skills and the *process*. The product is the output of the skill; what it is that the skills have been learned to produce. The process is the stages that the trainees went through in order to achieve the output. In some cases it is crucial that the trainees follow the exact procedure to achieve the task. These are likely to be when the consequences of performing differently might be dangerous or costly or when they are part of a procedure where other people might have to take over part-way through and be able to fit in with the previous person's method of operation. In other cases, it probably does not matter how the operator achieved the task, provided that it has been achieved within operating standards of time, cost and usage of material.

For physical skills, the feedback might be on the product, the process or both. For mental skills, however, the feedback will more than likely be on the product, as we cannot see how someone is working out problems in their head.

For social skills, on the other hand, the feedback will be on the process of how they carried out the interaction, rather than on the outcome of the meeting. The evaluation of the outcome will involve more than the social skills alone and will probably bring in some knowledge and judgement as well. As social skills are the skills of handling people, a major source of the effectiveness of those skills will be the people on the receiving end of the trainee's actions.

A key person in the feedback on the social skills of a trainee selection interviewer, for example, would be the candidate. The role cannot be filled successfully by external observers as they are not feeling the effects of the interviewer's behaviour. They would not have been in exactly the right seating position to experience the impact of the eye contact, facial expressions or the angle of the interviewer's body.

The person playing the part of the candidate has to be sensitive to the emotions they are experiencing, able to articulate them and able to analyse what in the interviewer's behaviour caused them. There are also merits in ensuring that the 'candidate' is someone skilled in giving feedback. All of these abilities in the 'candidate' demand a highly skilled person to play that role. These skills will probably be beyond those of another participant in the training programme. We shall consider, later, who should take this role.

After Judgement Sessions

When we distinguished feedback from debriefing we considered the legitimacy of providing feedback after a judgement session where there is no right or wrong answer. From the Training Techniques Matrix in Chapter 1, it can be seen that the usual vehicles for judgement training are discussions of trainees' own experiences, case studies and exercises.

Discussions

In the first of these, the trainees relate incidences from their past and if they say that it happened, then it happened! Feedback would not be appropriate, unless they were factually wrong in their recollection of an incident or unless their point was in no way relevant to the topic under discussion. If the latter does appear to be the case, it is more often than not a question of the powers of expression of the participant than of the content of what they are trying to say. A few questions from the instructor and a few examples from the trainee usually clarify.

For judgement discussions only debriefing, not feedback, can be used.

Geraldine, the training manager at Smithson's, designed a training session to enable managers to improve their ability in motivating their staff. She distinguished between the ideas that managers could use and their ability to implement these ideas. For the first part, she knew that the managers had a fair amount of experience of staff management between them and so selected a discussion as the appropriate training vehicle with the input coming from the participants' own backgrounds. She initiated the exchange of experiences with the question, 'What ways do you use to motivate your staff?'. From past situations in their working history, the discussion group described what had worked for them. Other participants investigated the circumstances and then learned new methods that they might decide to try on their own staff, with the assurance that this was not just theory but had actually proved successful for someone they knew.

Case Studies

In case studies, we are reviewing the trainees' ideas about how they might tackle a particular problem or what conclusions they would draw from past events.

Philip needed to train managers in his company in team-work and the particular need was to help newly appointed managers to handle staff matters among people who were previously their peers. For the judgement component, he felt that the trainees would not have sufficient experience to discuss the issues first hand, so he selected the following case study as the input.

'You are the sales manager and, as an incentive-cum-sales conference, you have taken your team of sales representatives to Malaysia. One night, or early in the morning, the hotel security manager informs you that some of your people are holding a rowdy party in a bedroom and that unless you can quieten them he will call the police. You go to the offending room to ask them to stop the noise and, to your horror, you see one of your staff taking heroin. What would you do? (Possession of more than 15 grammes of heroin in Malaysia carries a mandatory death penalty.)'

The chances of any participant being faced with this exact situation are, hopefully, zero, but the discussion will bring out very many issues which do have direct application in every manager's job, including:

- What is a manager's responsibility for staff conduct both in and out of working hours?
- Should managers implement rules that can mean severe punishment for their staff, when they may not necessarily agree with those rules?
- What effects, both positive and negative, does the enforcement of rules have on the morale of the team and their perception of their manager?
- Where are a manager's loyalties: to the team, to an individual on that team, to their own manager, to the good name of the company, to the law?
- What are your expectations of your own manager?

A common approach when using case studies is for syndicates of learners to consider their judgement and then to report back in plenary for comments from the trainer. As the session is designed to help participants to develop their thinking processes, the actual decision that they make is less important than the quality of the discussion in reaching that decision. Having announced their view, it is fairly typical for the learners to ask the trainers what they would do under the circumstances or, worse, what is the right answer. Of course, there is no right answer and for the trainers to suggest one would not only be misleading, it would also create a level of dependence on the trainers that judgement training tries to prevent. Believing that every management situation has a right answer and that someone somewhere holds it leads to indecision and prevarication that are not the qualities of good managers. Further, the participants will probably interpret the trainer's view as the company policy and will try to fit it to any even remotely related problem that they might meet subsequently.

When asked for their views, the trainers who say that they have none will have an adverse effect on the participants who might doubt their credibility to run the programme. A good method of achieving the balance is to describe those factors that the trainers would consider when trying to reach a decision and summarize some of the options available.

Often with such a case as this, which is designed to raise the emotional temperature, a follow-up case is used where a sales representative is discovered filling his spouse's car with petrol and charging it to the company account. The issues have been raised in the drug case and the application can be seen in the petrol one.

In judgement training the only time when it is appropriate to give feedback as opposed to debriefing is if the trainees make a mistake on knowledge: if they are incorrect on the company policy or the legal position. Under these circumstances, the trainees would be wrong and it is up to the instructors to ensure that the mistakes are rectified. If, for example, in the petrol case, a participant recommended instant dismissal on the petrol station forecourt, the trainers would point out that this was against company policy which states that there must always be an investigation before dismissal proceedings are considered.

The Group or Leadership Exercise

The Training Techniques Matrix in Chapter 1 shows that the purpose of the group exercise is primarily as an input for judgement. The training participants probably have too little first-hand experience of working in teams to be able to discuss the issues of teamwork from their own experience. The trainers have, therefore, decided that an exercise will give the participants some experience that can be used as an input for subsequent discussion about the options involved in team-working. Learners take part in the event, which might be as simple as a half-hour ranking exercise, agreeing the highest to the lowest significance of ten qualities of a good manager, to as complicated as a three-day adventure rescuing climbers from a wind-swept mountain range. Having taken part in the activity, participants are now in a first-hand position to discuss how it feels to be part of a team, the concepts of dependence on others, what constitutes leadership, how leadership is determined and so on. This would be a debriefing session. For managers who have been team members for many years, such an endeavour would be unnecessary as they would already have experienced these issues in real life. Clearly, for the trainees themselves, for the training to have relevance for their work and for the employer who is probably financing the process, the lessons learned must be transferable to the working environment.

It is possible for such group exercises to be used to develop the *skills* of working in teams or of leadership. However, the Training Techniques Matrix would recommend that there be a demonstration of the skills to be learned by a competent instructor and the exercise would then become a role play where each trainee, in turn, takes the role of leader and the others take the position of team members. The trainees could then receive feedback on their ability to implement the skills that had been demonstrated. In reality this is rarely done. To isolate the particular leadership skills to be demonstrated and practised would be the first requirement. The time taken for each participant to practise each skill and to receive feedback on that skill would probably make the length of the training programmes financially non-viable for most companies.

Questions must be asked, then, about the ethics of asking learners to take part in such an exercise, without any input of the skills that they are supposed to be practising and then giving them feedback on their ability to implement those skills. Presumably, if they were good at the skills to begin with, they would not need to be on the training course. If they are on the course, it is because their level of skills is not considered high enough. Practising the skills at their current, low level of competence, without an input of a better method, can only reproduce performance at that low level, leading to critical feedback more than praise. At best this will show the trainees the limitations of their current abilities, but this constitutes assessment or the identification of training needs rather than the training and development of new skills. Having spent time in this diagnostic phase, often there is too little time left for the trainee to learn the skills and develop competence and confidence. At worst it can lead to demoralization of the trainees and resentment against the trainers who put the trainees in this invidious position.

After Attitude Sessions

By their very nature, attitudes are internal to the individual and only show themselves through that person's behaviour. It is an assumption, therefore, that because someone is seen behaving in a certain way, that this definitely means that they hold a particular attitude. Sometimes this assumption can lead to embarrassing consequences which lower the trainer's credibility in the eyes of the trainees for all future feedback.

After a practice session on working in teams, Graham pointed out that at one stage in the meeting, Richard was so bored that he physically moved his chair away from the table and so distanced himself from the group and the proceedings. Graham even demonstrated this point on video by showing how Richard's chair was pushed back and actually disappeared from the television screen. On receiving this feedback Richard was quite puzzled and denied being at any time uninterested. When he saw the video replay, however, he remembered the incident exactly. The sun had been edging its way around the room and rather than disturb the meeting by standing up and drawing the curtains, he moved his chair back to avoid the glare!

It is not as common for companies to define attitude objectives for their training as it is for them to define knowledge, skills and judgement objectives. The attitude objectives are frequently left to the instructors to decide. A possible consequence of this is that the attitudes determined are those that are held by the instructors themselves. This leads to the subjective decision for feedback as to whether the attitudes which it is claimed that trainees hold are the same as those of the instructors. Under these conditions it will be very difficult for the trainers to retain the objectivity so necessary for effective feedback. To do so would mean knowing precisely their own attitudes on a subject and not allowing this to influence their feedback on other people's attitudes. If the trainer feels that his or her attitude is right, and most of us do feel that way about our own attitudes, then they might criticize any trainee who does not conform to their views.

A safer option has to be to keep the feedback in the realms of observable behaviour and leave the attitude analysis to the trainees themselves to deduce. After all, if the trainees exhibit the behaviour which is required, some would argue, their underlying attitudes and beliefs are up to them anyway.

The Role Play

The role play technique is one of the most widely used training methods in interpersonal skills training – and one of the most feared! The fear is usually based on first- or second-hand accounts of where the training has gone horribly wrong, trainees having been embarrassed, humiliated or reduced to tears of frustration or mirth. Some learners are known to report that they do not sleep the night before they know that they will be involved in role plays. The handling of the feedback from role plays can often be the cause.

The invention of the technique is usually credited to an Austrian psychotherapist, Josef Moreno, a student of Sigmund Freud. Moreno's (1953) belief was that the cause of some people's serious social skills difficulties could be traced back to events in their childhood or formative years when they were faced with an interpersonal or emotional problem that they could not handle. This might have been with a parent or a sibling and had such a detrimental effect on them that it has caused a blockage whenever they face similar situations in later life. If the psychotherapist can help the patient to identify the situation, they can devise ways that could have been used to handle the problem at the time. This will clear the blockage and the patient will be able to meet new situations with more confidence. The role play was the patient's opportunity to re-confront the difficult blockage. The patients might play themselves at the age that the incident arose and the therapist might play the parent or sibling.

This is a far cry from the needs of most of the participants who attend management and sales training programmes wanting to learn how to handle difficult staff or to improve their rate of overcoming objections from prospective customers.

The name, role play, is a complete misnomer for its current, popular use. There should be no question of 'play' as training is a serious and expensive business. Nor are we asking the trainees to play a 'role'. The position that the trainees are in is an opportunity to practise certain skills and, as such, there would be little value in practising how someone else might handle the situation. The trainees should be themselves and only the context of the practice might be a little artificial. Replacing the term 'role play' with 'practice' takes much of the mystique and fear from the trainees and the success of the sessions increases dramatically.

The purpose of the role play is two-fold. First, to practise certain social skills and second, and quite separately, to consider the factors involved in making decisions in various interpersonal interactions. This, latter, we have been calling judgement. In every conversation with another person we are doing both of these together: deciding what to say (judgement) and then saying it (social skill). Feedback is only legitimate when reviewing with the trainees how successful they were at conveying the message that they had decided to convey. The trainer's function is to help the trainees to realize how their message is affected by the actual words they used, by the tones of voice and by the gestures. Stressing different words in the same sentence can convey quite different meanings.

EXERCISE

Read the following sentence aloud eight times and each time emphasize a different word in the sentence. Consider the different meanings that the listener would interpret from each reading:
  'I didn't say that he stole the money.'

In our interactions with other people, we are operating in two areas. First, we are deciding how to handle the situation and what to say. This is a judgement, unless we are simply following rules, in which case it is knowledge. Second, we are actually saying the words and using the body language to communicate the message. This is the social skill. For feedback after a role play to be really effective, it is essential that the judgement is separated from the social skill. The decisions to be implemented should be discussed, and those judgements debriefed before the role play takes place so that the trainees know what they are trying to achieve. Then would follow the role play which is a very short practice at the social skill of implementing that decision. The best role plays, or practice sessions, last less than a minute. Were they to last any longer, the trainees would be moved into a position where they were having to make more judgements and this will cloud the review.

> The participants discussed the various ways of handling a complaining customer. As there were no company guidelines on this, each trainee was being trained in using their discretion. This was the judgement. Jamie's decision was to tell the customer that there would be no refund as the items had been used before being returned. In the role play he practised doing this in a socially skilled way that did not offend the customer.

Because of the criticality of tones of voice, eye contact, facial expressions and body movement, the person giving the feedback must have been on the direct receiving end of the trainee's conversation; that is, they must be the other role player. This person must have the sensitivity to be able to feel the effects of the interviewer's comments, remember what caused them and be skilled in facilitating the feedback to the trainee. To fulfil this extremely taxing role needs a highly skilled professional and the only person in the training room who is probably going to be able to meet these demands is the trainer. An added advantage of having the trainer play one of the parts is that there is no chance of the role play getting out of hand. It has been known for trainees who have been niggling each other during the training to view the role play as a licensed opportunity to argue. Further, if the trainee practising the skills appears to be having difficulty, the trainer, in role, can provide help by giving continuous feedback during the practice. In a selection interview practice, for example, the trainer, in the role of the candidate, can comment that a particularly good question was asked. If the trainee interviewer gets stuck for a question, the candidate can volunteer a new area for exploration: 'Would it help if I told you what I do in my current job?'.

Whilst this approach may differ from that used by some trainers, the advantages justify it over having another participant as the other role player with all of the unpredictability that that can bring. Training is an important and expensive business and the more accidents and unpredictability can be designed out, the more effective it will be.

Once we have separated the judgement from the social skills, the Training Techniques Matrix will advise on the best way to teach the social skills component. The input will come from a demonstration by the trainer of the skills to be learned, the process will be by practice and the output will be the performance by the trainee of the skill. This output can then be compared with the input demonstration and feedback can be given about which parts of the skill were performed to the requisite standard, which parts did not achieve that standard and why and what can be done to improve for the next practice.

Review

Feedback has its place in both on- and off-the-job training situations. The type of feedback will depend upon the type of learning, knowledge, skills, judgement and attitudes. Particular care must be taken when giving feedback after role plays and group exercises so that it is focused on the skills being developed and not the judgements being made.

CHECKLIST FOR THE TRAINER

- What is determining whether you are running training 'on-the-job' or 'off-the-job'?
- Is your feedback after skills sessions focusing on 'product', 'process' or both?
- Are your role plays and exercises for training purposes or for assessment and diagnostic purposes?
- Are you attempting to change attitudes in your training?
- If so, what are your training objectives and measurement criteria?

---

4 How to Give Feedback

	SUMMARY	
▷		◁

This chapter:
- looks at two traits of the instructor that lead to more effective feedback;
- describes the different styles of feedback;
- suggests who should give feedback – and who should not;
- considers the use of observers and video cameras in feedback;
- gives ten rules for giving feedback;
- discusses when to give feedback – and when not to;
- reviews where to give the feedback;
- gives a formula for giving feedback – and one to avoid.

From the previous classification, we saw that feedback is applicable mainly to knowledge and skills. Judgement is related to debriefing and attitudes are not observable. Giving effective feedback is not easy and much thought has to go into planning why, who, how, what, when and where. The traits of the trainer and the styles of feedback are also significant.

Two Traits of the Instructor

The relationship between trainer and trainees will affect how the feedback is received and two important traits of the instructor will help to determine whether or not the feedback is accepted. These are the credibility and the identification of the trainer.

Credibility

It is rather a cyclic argument, but the trainer's feedback will only be believed if the trainer is believable. This credibility should be in both the technical aspects of the knowledge and skills being taught and the training aspects of managing the training event. Probably the best way for the instructors to prove their credibility is to demonstrate the skills that they are teaching. If they carry out the input demonstration, rather than rely on a video of someone else doing it – or worse, not have an input demonstration at all – they clearly have the technical credibility. Their demonstration should not be at the highest possible level of the skill, but at the standard that they want the trainees to achieve. If the level demonstrated by the instructors is too high, it will only serve to distance them from the learners who will feel that they are being asked to achieve the impossible. As the learners' own competence at a skill improves, so the demonstrations by the instructors will be at a higher level.

Identification

The instructors' feedback will also be more effective if they can identify with the learners and vice versa. If the trainers can relate to the learners' circumstances, their feedback will be more readily accepted. The identification will be achieved by the trainers finding out as much as possible about the trainees' working environments and the conditions under which they will be using these new skills in real life. The identification will also be established by the trainers recognizing, and responding to, the emotions of the learners during the training. Discussing how the trainees are feeling, their concerns and apprehensions, is an important part of the process, especially if the participants are able to share these views.

Different Styles of Feedback

The Direct Style

Supporters of a direct approach to feedback, like myself, would argue that for feedback in the area of knowledge, there can be no doubt – the trainee was right or was wrong and if they were wrong, it is important that they are told that they are wrong so that there can be no confusion next time. Feedback has nothing to do with punishing, embarrassing or humiliating the trainees, so it is with no sense of vindictiveness that the errors are described and corrected. Caring instructors will want their learners to succeed and only direct, objective, unambiguous feedback will clarify what the knowledge really is. The trainers have the knowledge; that is why they have been selected to train. The trainees do not; that is what they have come to learn. When a question of knowledge is raised by a trainee there is little point in the tutor throwing it open for the other participants to answer. If the rest of the trainees do know the answer, the trainee who did not is isolated. If the rest do not know the answer, the time spent in asking them has been wasted. Unfortunately, a device used in schools by weak teachers was to ask the class to think of the answer, so as to give the teacher thinking time to recall it. If that failed and the teacher still did not know, discovery of the answer was set as homework. The trainees of today are too bright to fall for these ruses.

The Indirect Style

A style advocated by some trainers is to be less direct. They claim that trainees learn best when they are able to extract what they want to learn from a supportive environment. For the tutor to be the font of the feedback might establish a sense of dependence on the tutor which may not be easy to release at the end of the training. There is also the risk that the relationship between teacher and taught could be soured if the learner takes offence at the feedback. If the trainers remain neutral and distanced from the feedback being given, they are able to intervene to protect the trainee should that be necessary. In this indirect style, the feedback would come from a variety of sources including the trainees themselves, observers or video. The trainees could accept or reject the feedback they are offered and so take responsibility for their own learning.

Proponents of the indirect style of feedback recommend that the comments come from the other participants as they are then easier for the individual learner to accept or reject than if they came from the tutor. The fans of direct feedback would argue that if the feedback is too easy for the trainees to reject, there seems little point in giving it to them in the first place. Sometimes the weight of the instructor behind the comments is necessary for the trainees to listen and learn. Certainly, the other trainees can learn a great deal from watching their fellows and viewing their successes and failures. They can also learn from the decisions involved in each incident and this can act as an excellent input for the debrief. However, using the observers to give feedback as well is another matter, as we shall discuss shortly.

A Middle Road

As with many things in life, there is a middle road where the trainer mixes the direct and indirect styles. To avoid any confusion of relationships with the tutor among the participants, the trainers will usually begin the feedback in the indirect style and then come in themselves towards the end. Their contributions will probably be for the sake of balance or to pick up important issues that had not been mentioned before or sufficiently emphasized. This middle road may carry the best of both styles or may miss the benefits of each.

Who Should Give the Feedback

Anyone who has witnessed the training sessions could be in a position to give feedback, but it is the trainer and the trainee who has actually been practising who are best equipped.

The Trainer

It is the trainer who is the source of competence in the knowledge or the skills being learned and it is the trainer who has demonstrated these skills to the learners. One of the best people, therefore, to give feedback after the trainees' attempts is the trainer. As instructors, their competence should be twofold; first, in the knowledge and skills to be taught and second, in the trainer skills of giving feedback and judging when the trainees have had sufficient. They know what to look for and how to explain it. They also know some of the best ways of helping the trainees to improve their performance.

The Trainees Themselves

The trainee who has actually been undergoing the practice or the test is in a very strong position to describe how he or she felt, what they found difficult and what they found easy. It would be ignoring a great resource if this trainee was not brought in to discuss their own performance. Focusing on the practising trainees also demonstrates that they are the key figures in the process, that it is for their benefit and that their commitment is essential. It is always a good format, even using the direct style, to begin the feedback by asking the practising trainees how they felt the exercise went. To prevent the repetition of, 'How do you feel that went?', various questions, with similar purposes can be asked:

> 'What is your reaction to the exercise?'
> 'How happy are you with that?'
> 'How much did that differ from your plan?'
> 'What, if anything, did you find difficult about that?'
> 'What particular skills were you concentrating on?'

The trainees' answers will serve to reinforce that they are the centre of attention and will act as a barometer of how receptive they will be to the feedback, as we shall see in the next chapter.

Most trainees are fairly aware of their performance at a test or exercise and are able to describe those areas where they feel they need guidance. Encouraging the learner to identify these trouble spots enables the trainer to structure the order in which points are covered. Some trainees, when asked about their performance, cannot or will not reflect on it. In the next chapter we shall discuss why this might be and what to do about it.

The Use of Other Trainees as Observers

Trainees on a training course, other than when they are practising, have often been used as observers in feedback sessions for two reasons. First, they were used for recording what happened and acted as extra pairs of eyes and ears; second, trainers were not quite sure what to do with the other trainees who were awaiting their turn to practise. Rather than have them sitting around getting apprehensive or bored, it was felt that asking them to observe and make notes would give them something useful to do. It has also been suggested that if the feedback comes from peers rather than from the trainers, it would be easier for the students to accept or reject.

The validity of these reasons is now considered suspect. Other trainees are not always accurate in their observations and this can cause faulty or misleading feedback. They can make errors in their recollections of the actual words and phrases that were used and can thus entirely invalidate the feedback. Video and audio recording is significantly more reliable at noting what actually did happen and the words, tones and body language used.

The other trainees are not always skilled at giving feedback, either. They can be evaluative rather than objective and sometimes fall into the game of 'mutual niceness' when trainees say positive platitudes about colleagues as an investment for when it is their turn! On the other hand, occasionally, there can be licence for one trainee to abuse another.

If there are several observers called upon to comment, it is highly likely that they will all notice the same points. This can lead to excessive feedback as each makes their observations. The excess could be caused by several observers each making different criticisms or the same criticism being made several times. When the other participants are asked to observe, some people do so with amazing detail and record every word, phrase and raised eyebrow that they saw. It could be that during the account from one observer, the trainer judges that the trainee has received sufficient feedback. The tutor is then faced with the dilemma of cutting off an observer who still has four more pages of detail to report or allowing the practising trainee to be hurt.

If instructors can be clear about the precise skills that they want their trainees to practise, they can design practice sessions that are targeted at exactly that skill and that are kept very short. This minimizes the time that the other trainees are not directly involved and so limits their boredom. If each practice session can be slightly different, yet still maintain the focus on the key skills, the participants' interest can be held.

Should it be felt necessary to use observers, it is helpful to issue them with observation sheets with lists of questions. To prevent repetition, the observation sheets should all be different. To prevent too much criticism the questions should be biased to record points for potential praise, and to prevent evaluations, the questions should ask the observers to note specific words and phrases used.

Jackie was concerned about the feedback sessions after each of her trainee selection interviewers conducted a role play. She would have dearly loved to have a co-trainer so that the trainee interviewer could go into a separate room with the co-trainer and a video tape of the interview and review the skills in detail. Unfortunately, time and budgets meant that she had to supervise all the practices herself. To prevent the problems of enthusiastic but amateur observers, she produced observation sheets for the other trainees to cover each skill.

The first questioning observation sheet asked an observer to record the actual words of all the open-ended questions that were asked. By asking for examples of open-ended questions, which was one of the skills being practised, the comments from the observer could only lead to praise, unless no open-ended questions were asked at all! The second questioning observation sheet asked an observer to record the actual words of all the closed questions that were asked. The listening sheet asked for examples of active listening. Jackie knew that the number of observations made would probably be well in excess of the number of criticisms that the trainee would be able to accept, so she warned the observers that they would not be called upon to report all of their notes.

OBSERVATION SHEETS FOR INTERVIEWING

Introduction

To help us to give feedback to your colleagues who are practising their interviewing skills, it would be useful to have an accurate record of what was said during the interview. Could you please write down the observations that you are asked to make about what the interviewer said and did. Try to be as precise as you can, as it is the actual words and phrases that make all the difference. After the role play, the instructor will ask you for some of the examples, but may not necessarily call upon you to report all of your observations. When you are asked, please just present your observations and try not to evaluate them as being good or bad. During the feedback session we shall judge the merits of each point.

Observation Sheet 1 Open-ended questions

Please write down the actual open-ended questions that the interviewer asked.

Open-ended question 1 _____

_____

Open-ended question 2 _____

_____

Open-ended question 3 _____

_____

Observation Sheet 2 Closed questions

Please write down the actual closed questions that the interviewer asked.

Closed question 1 _____

_____

Closed question 2 _____

_____

Closed question 3 _____

_____

Observation Sheet 3   Listening skills
Please write down actual examples of the indicators that showed you that the interviewer was listening. These indicators might include head and body movements, facial expressions or words and phrases.

Head movements   _____

_____

Body movements   _____

_____

Facial expressions   _____

_____

Words and phrases   _____

_____

Video and Audio Recordings

'The camera never lies', is a well worn aphorism which is almost true when it comes to video taping practical sessions in training. Certainly the lens does record what it sees, though camera angles can distort the view and what is played back may have a bias over what was seen by those present. The lens is objective in what it sees, but only uses one 'eye'. A video recording is therefore always going to appear less interesting than a human observation using stereoscopic vision.

Modern video cameras used in training have the feature of a zoom lens, though this must be used with caution. Using the zoom lens demands the presence of a camera operator. Most trainees quickly forget about the presence of the camera when it is left running unattended, but this is much harder when someone is standing behind it. Older cameras can have such a noisy motor to operate the zoom that the trainees are distracted, wondering what they have done that is being magnified.

Operating the zoom lens can be extremely boring and it takes great willpower for the operator to resist highlighting points for amusement, rather than learning, value. The play back of the tape also has potential dangers. The recording of the images is objective in that it actually happened, but the overriding of this by a camera operator with a zoom lens now introduces subjectivity. Unless it is important to note the smallest detail, it is probably advisable to use the video purely to record and to refresh memories, and to minimize the use of the zoom.

Playing back the whole tape of a practical session can be time-consuming and tedious. When playing back only selections from the video tape, trainers must ensure that they do not bias the impression of the whole exercise by choosing only the parts that went well or did not go well. Balance must be maintained.

Finding the particular point to be highlighted from the whole tape is not always easy and valuable time can be spent searching the tape while the trainees lose interest. An accurate and visible counter on the machines obviously helps. If the practice sessions are kept short, there is less tape to search. If the trainers play one of the parts in the role play they will be on camera. With a little planning, they can devise a series of signals, slight body movements, that will be on the tape and can be found readily by searching the tape. A raised finger might indicate an open question was asked or a scratched nose might mean an example of active listening.

To maintain the supportive climate for the feedback, it helps if the trainers can sit in the group with the participants, preferably next to the trainee who is receiving the feedback. Infra-red remote control units for the video and the television monitor are extremely good for facilitating this.

Audio tapes can be useful for playing back conversations and are ideal for feedback on telephone techniques when the faces and body language of the participants could not be seen anyway. However, much face-to-face communication is more non-verbal than verbal and audio tapes will give a misleading account of the true interaction.

Television programmes showing the out-takes, when a production went embarrassingly wrong, make very entertaining viewing, but do sometimes worry trainees that tapes of their performance might turn up at an office party. At the end of the training programme it is advisable to re-assure the trainees by wiping the tapes clean or, better still, giving their tapes to the participants. The keen ones might even review their learning at home after the course!

```
┌─────────────────────────────────────────────────────────────┐
│                                                             │
│           Ten Rules for Giving Feedback                     │
│                                                             │
│           1.   It should be balanced                        │
│           2.   It should be specific                        │
│           3.   It should be objective                       │
│           4.   It should be appropriate                     │
│           5.   It should be understandable                  │
│           6.   It should be participative                   │
│           7.   It should be comparable                      │
│           8.   It should be actionable                      │
│           9.   It should be sufficient                      │
│          10.   It should be hierarchical                    │
│                                                             │
└─────────────────────────────────────────────────────────────┘
```

1. It Should Be Balanced

The trainees should recognize that the feedback is designed to help them to learn and to improve their performance. If the feedback is too critical the students might resent it and if it is too praising, they might reject it as being patronizing. The comments made should be a balance of praise and criticism, though every point must be genuine and worth making. This balance does not mean that praise should be alternated with criticism. If trainees can see any sort of pattern they will become suspicious. The order of praise and criticism should be mixed up so that the trainee can never anticipate which is to come next. That way they will listen to each point with equal attention.

To help the instructor achieve this balance, it is often useful to keep notes of the trainee's performance on a sheet of paper divided down the middle with the positive points in one column and the negative ones in the other. When using video, it can simply be a case of listing the counter number of points in each column. Alternatively, the trainer may well develop a set of personal codes that can be marked next to observations. If the trainee sees the trainer's notes lying on the table or can see them during the session, it might not help if the distinction between the good and the bad points is too obvious, particularly if one column is significantly longer than the other! A very easy way of disguising the list is to put a full stop after the positive comments or video counter numbers and to omit it from the negative ones. The comments would then be listed vertically without columns and the distinction would only be noticeable to the trainer.

The ratio of praise to criticism that a trainee can take is a function of several variables including the personality of the trainees, their culture and the privacy of the feedback. These variables are discussed in the next chapter.

2. It Should Be Specific

There should be no argument as to whether the trainee did or did not do or say the points under review. The trainer should be able to refer to the specific issue and recount exactly what happened. Obviously, video or audio recording helps considerably in this task and can even reproduce the tone of voice that was used if this is significant. Using the video counter number or making signals to the camera during the recording enables the exact point to be found quickly. The instructor can use a shorthand to indicate next to their record of the counter number what the incident was. For example, they could put a 'q' next to the counter number for a question or an 'l' for an example of listening.

TRAINER'S OBSERVATION SHEET FOR A VIDEO RECORDED INTERVIEW PRACTICE

The number shows the point on the video tape; the letter shows the skill being observed; the full stop indicates a good example; absence of a full stop shows a poor example.

23 oq.   (a good open-ended question)
48L   (a poor example of listening)
69 cq.   (a good example of a closed question)
94 s   (a poor summary).

It is best to avoid phrases like, 'You tended to …' or 'You were always …' as these are generalizations and the trainees will probably be able to counter the comments with times when they did not do or say what you are suggesting.

3. It Should Be Objective

It is not up to the instructor to be evaluative about the behaviour of the trainee. The feedback should be factual as to what exactly happened and the positive or negative effect of this behaviour. For example, 'When you asked, "Are you ambitious?" the answer you received was the single word, "Yes"', is preferable to, 'You asked a lot of closed questions which didn't produce very much.' Again, video can show the facts of what happened and the results. In a role play, if the trainers are playing one of the parts, they can say, factually, how they felt as a result of the trainee's actions. It would be fair, under those circumstances, for the trainer to say, 'When you asked, "Do you and your partner intend starting a family?", I felt that you were intruding into my personal life.' The feedback enables the trainees to realize the effect of their behaviour on the other person. This can then be matched with the decision on how the trainee wanted the 'interviewee' to feel. If it was their judgement that they wanted the interviewee to feel stressed by a certain question, the feedback would show whether or not they succeeded. A subsequent debrief would discuss the relative advantages and situations when it might be appropriate and inappropriate to stress a candidate. If the company policy was that stress questions should never be used in an interview, then the trainee was wrong as they have gone against the knowledge of the company rules. They would, thus, receive feedback from the instructor that they were wrong, why it was wrong and what they should have said.

4. It Should Be Appropriate

In the practice session, the trainees know exactly what skills they are trying to develop and it is in these areas that they are expecting to receive feedback. They will, of course, have been studying the input of the knowledge or skills from the teacher anyway. While it might be legitimate for the trainer to give feedback in other areas, if these are significant, it is not fair to comment on trivial points. This will come across as petty and will devalue the proper feedback which is being given. If the session is to practise listening skills, it would be appropriate for the trainer to comment on the interviewer's facial expression, but it would not be appropriate to mention mannerisms unrelated to listening.

In Chapter 1 we discussed a model of learning which showed that there should be an input, a process and an output stage for the learning to be complete. The input stage would be a demonstration of the skill, the process would be the practice of that skill and the output would be what the trainer observes the learner doing. In preparation for their practice, the trainees will be revising the particular knowledge or skills for that session. They are bound to feel cheated if they receive feedback in other areas, like a school student given an examination question on points outside the syllabus.

5. It Should Be Understandable

For some trainees, receiving feedback can be a rather uncomfortable experience, not particularly because the content is threatening, but sometimes because the individual does not like being under the spotlight. For these people, the quicker the session is over, the better. It is important, therefore, that the tutor makes the feedback fully comprehensible to the learner, as seeking clarification will only prolong the discomfort. The trainees might just nod and say that they understand. In some cases, if the trainee does ask the trainer to develop what they are saying, this might be misconstrued as disagreement or insolence by the trainee. The language that the instructor uses should be clearly understood by the learner. It is important that the trainers limit the amount of jargon that they use in the feedback. Although they may have described certain models and theories to the trainees, the trainees will not be as conversant as their trainers.

> After her role play during an interpersonal skills course, Sarah was told that her critical parent style was causing Peter to behave as an adaptive child. Although the principles of transactional analysis had been mentioned, it took Sarah a while to understand exactly what was meant. She was nervous about asking as it might have shown up her problems of understanding the theory sessions as well as practising the skills.

Video playback is extremely helpful again to explain exactly what did happen and demonstrations by the trainer will cover exactly what should happen.

6. It Should Be Participative

For the feedback to be successful, there must be a commitment from the trainees to want to try the new behaviours that are being suggested. This means that the learners should be involved in the ideas for change. Of course, the trainees themselves cannot always know what is the best course of action for them to take. That is one of the reasons that they are consulting the expertise of the instructor. They should not feel, however, that the suggestion is imposed on them without regard to their view of their capability of implementing it. We have already discussed why it is useful for the trainee to make the first comments on their performance; if they have an immediate opportunity to try out the new approach and to see that it does work for them, their commitment will be cemented there and then.

7. It Should Be Comparable

Progress is made when the trainees can compare their current performance with the previous attempts. For this reason, the feedback should be comparable with previous sessions. If the trainer criticized their questioning technique after the first interview practice, this is exactly the area for comment after the next practice. The trainee will have been concentrating on this skill and will probably show an improvement anyway, so that it is an opportunity for praise. Instructors who think that they will be perceived as nagging about the same points are doing a disservice to their trainees. As part of the briefing for the exercise, it is a good idea to clarify with the trainee exactly what are the skills that they are trying to practise and the level of competence that they are trying to achieve. A few minutes later, after the practice, their performance can be compared with their objectives.

8. It Should Be Actionable

There is little point in giving trainees information about which they can do nothing. If the learners are tall, short, limp or stutter, they already know about it anyway and it is insulting for the instructor to highlight it. The purpose of feedback is to help people to learn and the feedback must not only highlight just those areas where the person can learn, it must also include an agreed course of action that the student can follow. Sometimes the action suggested by the trainers might be suitable for themselves and for many other trainees, but is outside the repertoire of this particular student. It could be as basic as the trainer being right handed and the student being left handed, so when the student is advised to push harder with the right hand, there is simply no strength left. An observant and experienced instructor will notice the difficulties that the learner is having and will agree plans that are within the learner's capabilities.

There is little point in telling a trainee who is practising handling meetings to 'Be more assertive' in dealing with a repetitive team member. The advice given to help the trainee to improve must specify the actual behaviour that he or she should try. The suggestion would be better phrased as, 'Try standing up and writing a summary on the whiteboard as this will indicate that the issue has been discussed and will prevent the person repeating the same point.' A quick re-enactment of the same scene will give the learner the chance to try out the new approach and to see if they feel able to use it.

9. It Should Be Sufficient

Trainees work hard in preparation for practice sessions and tests and commit a great deal of effort during the process. To reflect this effort, the tutor must spend a reasonable period of time with each trainee reviewing performance. If too little time is spent, the trainees will feel that the efforts have not been recognized and they might not feel so inclined to work that hard again. This is particularly true if the performance was good and there is not much to criticize. The better the performance, the harder the trainees have probably worked and the greater the need for recognition of effort. This is also an opportunity to catch them doing things right, which is the most efficient form of feedback there is.

Even if the trainee's session was appalling, there should be some time spent on the review, as to do otherwise would suggest that the trainers might want to ignore the trainee as well as their performance.

If there were several areas for criticism, trainers might want to limit the number covered to protect the trainees. Ideally the review of each trainee's practice should take roughly the same length of time. How this can be achieved is discussed later in this chapter.

10. It Should Be Hierarchical

There is a limit to how much criticism each trainee can take and this is often in the region of only three or four points. If the feedback is given sequentially, it could be that the trainees' threshold is reached before the really important criticisms have been made. If, however, the feedback is given hierarchically, the most significant point will be covered first, then the second most important point and so on. If the threshold is reached by the fourth point, it is less of a problem if feedback is not given on the more minor errors. These can always be picked up at another stage and will probably be rectified by the trainees anyway as they see other learners making the same mistakes and being coached on them.

Another reason for the hierarchical approach is the way our memories work. Whenever we are exposed to a new situation we tend to remember what happened at the beginning fairly well, and we can remember extremely well what happened at the end, but our recall of the middle period can be rather hazy. This is known as the 'primacy and recency effect' and is shown below.

It is this effect which accounts for the best act of a variety show being put on last and the second best act being put on first. In this way, if members of the audience were questioned several days after the show, they would be able to recall the best two acts most clearly.

In feedback, trainees will recall clearly the first item that they receive and, if this is also the most important point, it should be well learned. They will retain best the last point of feedback given (although we might have to forsake this benefit for the reasons explained in Chapter 6).

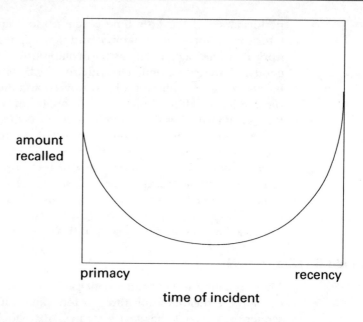

primacy   recency

time of incident

Figure 4.1 *How recall is affected by the time of the occurrence*

When to Give Feedback

There was a time when it was accepted wisdom that trainees wanted immediate knowledge of results. This is now considered too simplistic. Trainees need time to compose themselves before they are in the best condition to listen to and discuss a review of their performance. The greater the emotional involvement in the exercise, the longer the trainees need to 'let off steam'. For simple sessions, this might only be a matter of a couple of minutes. If there is more tension, a coffee break might be more in order. For school examinations, that might affect the student's whole life, three months is probably excessive, but errs on the right side!

At a European college for retail studies, students completed a two-year course on retail management which culminated in an end of course examination. Passing or failing the examination would have repercussions for the students' careers and, conceivably, for the rest of their lives. The examination consisted of around 200 objective test items of the true/false, multiple choice and matching types. Each student was issued with a question book and an answer key pad on which they entered the question number and their choice of answers. At the end of the two-hour test, the invigilator announced 'time' and disconnected the electrical supply to the answer pads – no writing another sentence to gain the extra marks here! She made a two-minute closing speech to the students and wished them well in their future careers. She then invited the students to leave the examination hall as their diplomas or reject slips were waiting for them. Having analysed their answers, the computer connected to the printer had been busy. As might be expected, it was several minutes before the first students walked nervously towards the door of the hall to read their fate.

Nearly always, trainees let off steam by themselves by laughing, sighing deeply or making a joke. If it does not happen naturally, the instructor should facilitate it or the tensions might still be around and will block the feedback. A joke, a smile and a few words of thanks are often sufficient. It will not help the tutor's job of giving feedback if they allow themselves to introduce evaluations into those words of thanks. If the trainers say, 'Well done, that was really good', they have given an assessment which may not be supported by their subsequent feedback. The trainee will then be confused, dilute the meaning of any criticisms or be suspicious of further comments from the trainer.

Where to Give Feedback

The more private the setting for the feedback, the more can be covered and ideally the feedback should be one-to-one in a quiet room with no audience. This is certainly possible in on-the-job training and coaching, but is less available on a training course when there are likely to be other participants present. When there are others around, regard has to be given to the esteem of the individual in front of colleagues. We shall discuss later how to set up a supportive atmosphere in such circumstances. On training courses, it is often possible to catch a few minutes with a trainee over a refreshment break. The break chosen, however, should not be too long after the trainee's session or the feedback will be too late. The impact on the other participants of taking this trainee aside will also have to be considered as they might feel that the individual is being separated from their support group. To enable the trainees to initiate further discussion on their performance, it is often helpful for the trainer to be available after hours. One of the real benefits of residential training is that there is no pressure on trainers or trainees to have to rush to catch transport home.

When receiving feedback in the actual training room, some participants like to remain where the skill took place and stay in that seat until the feedback is over. The advantages of this are that the trainee will be better able to remember instances as they will associate the location with the event. If the feedback does become excessive, they are also able to escape to their original chair which has the safety of being in the location that they established earlier in the training. The advantages of moving to their original chair straight after the practice and before the feedback is that this is one way of letting off steam and also enables the trainee to reflect on his or her performance more objectively from a neutral position. As the advantages of staying or moving are probably comparable, it is as well to allow the trainee to decide.

Feedback Formulae

There are two formulae that are often used when giving feedback; one is to be recommended, the other avoided.

THE FEEDBACK FORMULA THAT SHOULD BE USED

1. Let the trainees see what they have done
2. Let them see the effect of their behaviour
3. 'Agree' a change

---

1. Let the trainees see what they have done
By telling them, or showing them on video, what it is that they have done, the feedback will be objective, specific, understandable and non-evaluative.

2. Let them see the effect of their behaviour
By seeing a specific tangible effect of their action, trainees can learn and decide if their action has achieved what they wanted. Here there can be some evaluation from the trainer, though it should be supported with evidence.

3. 'Agree' a change
The trainer and trainee discuss alternative courses of action to prevent a recurrence. The 'agree' includes the trainer giving direct advice to, at the other extreme, the trainee making all the suggestions. Between these poles is a discussion of options by both parties. Ideally, having agreed a change, the trainee should have the immediate opportunity to imple-

ment it by trying the operation again. If practice sessions can be kept focused and short, there should be sufficient time. The effect on the trainees of now getting it right will boost their confidence, consolidate the learning and increase the chances of the learning being implemented in future. It will attract praise for the trainee and stimulate the desire for more learning. It is also extremely motivating for the trainers when they have tangible evidence that they are having a positive impact in their work!

Clearly, if the feedback is positive, there is no need for stage 3. For praise, the tutor simply identifies what the learner did and describes why it was successful. In this way the behaviour is reinforced and substantiated with the evidence of a positive outcome, which is more effective than highlighting the behaviour alone. Because praising people involves only two stages of the Feedback Formula rather than three, it justifies again the merits of catching people doing things right.

If trainees recognise that the instructor is using any type of formula on them, they are likely to resent what they might consider to be manipulation. To disguise this, tutors can vary the order in which they cover the two stages of the praising formula or three stages of the criticizing formula. So the feedback for praise, when practising the non-verbal skills of listening, might be:

1. When you leant towards me
2. I felt that you were really interested in what I was saying

Or:

2. I felt that you were really interested in what I was saying
1. when you leant towards me.

The 'agree' also includes feedback for criticism, which when practising open-ended questions in a selection interview, might be:

1. When you asked, 'Are you ambitious?',
2. the interviewee answered, 'Yes'.
3. How do you think you could re-phrase this question?

Or:

2. The interviewee answered, 'Yes'
1. when you asked, 'Are you ambitious?'
3. How do you think you could re-phrase this question?

Or:

3. How do you think you could re-phrase the question,
2. because the interviewee answered, 'Yes',
1. when you asked, 'Are you ambitious?'

By changing the order of the stages, the trainees will not see any pattern.

The Feedback Formula that Should Not Be Used

Another formula that is commonly used is the 'praise-criticize-praise sandwich'. The instructor tells the trainee something good, slips in the bad news and then ends on a high note. This formula has been in existence since primary school and has been experienced by most trainees countless times. Because it is so frequently used, there is a concern that it has become as transparent as a pane of glass and that bright trainees will see right through it. They know that the first praise is designed to soften them up, the truth is the middle part and the final praise is so that they do not go away feeling too bad. For example:

Praise: Your listening skills were good,
Criticize: but the questions were rather leading.
Praise: However, there was excellent eye contact.

It is possible that the reason that trainers have used this formula over the years is so that they do not feel too guilty in criticizing trainees. Learners who do recognize the formula will feel insulted that they are being treated like children and will suspect the validity of any of the feedback that they receive.

Words that Should Not Be Used

It is a useful maxim to remember that if there is the word 'but' in a feedback sentence, disregard everything that is said before the word 'but'. The word should never be used in feedback as it clearly combines two pieces of feedback, one of which is praising and the other criticizing. This will confuse the trainee and possibly dilute the impact of both comments. If there is more than one comment to make, these should be separated into different sentences and a full stop inserted between points. For example:

When you nodded and looked at me as I was speaking I really felt that you were interested in what I was saying. Another point that I want to make is that I was confused when you asked if I had children as I couldn't see the relevance of the question. Perhaps you could have asked what problems, if any, frequent nights away from home might cause me.

In addition to the word 'but', the following words should rarely appear in feedback sentences as they might have the same detrimental effect:

however, though, although, despite, nevertheless, nonetheless, yet, in spite of, notwithstanding, regardless, at any rate.

Equally, if a point is worth mentioning it must be significant. Therefore there should be no belittling of the issues. Phrases such as: 'just a minor point, barely worth raising' should be avoided. If it is 'barely worth raising' the trainer should not be wasting valuable training time on trivia. If it is worth mentioning, the trainer should give the issue the same importance as the other comments.

The Sequence for Giving Feedback

We have discussed a number of the very important issues involved in giving feedback, so it is worth putting these together in the typical sequence that a skills session might take.

1. *Demonstration and explanation of the skills by the instructor.*
This will be to the standard required of the trainee. It will set the standard and show that the trainer is credible. It will also enable the trainees to see exactly what they have to do and so focus their attention and minimize their apprehensions.

2. *Briefing on the practical sessions*
This will ensure that everyone knows what they are to do and further help to relieve any concerns. 'Theorists' will want more explanation behind the skills, 'Reflectors' will want time to think and consolidate their ideas, 'Pragmatists' will want to be sure of the details in the skill and 'Activists' will be ready to practise.

3. *Practical session by the first trainee*
The first participant practises the skills, while the others watch. The session should be short enough that it enables practice without becoming tedious for the observers or stressful for the practising participant. Observers might use observer sheets, if other means of recording are not available.

4. *Trainee 'lets off steam'*
A short break of a few seconds or, if necessary, minutes, enables the trainee to calm down and become receptive to the feedback. The trainer might well thank the trainee for his or her efforts, but should avoid saying that it was well done, particularly if it was not and the trainer is about to give some criticism.

5. *Trainee is asked how they feel the session went*
This focuses on the key player and allows the instructor to gauge the trainee's capacity for feedback, as we shall explore later. Areas that the trainee highlights as difficult are probably the ones that the trainer will start with.

6. *Conversation about the performance continues*
The trainer will be using the ten rules of feedback and the feedback formula for both praise and criticism and will be bringing in any observers or using the video to show what the trainee actually did say or do. In the direct style of feedback, the instructor will be leading the conversation by introducing each skill and giving feedback on the trainee's performance at each skill. In the indirect style, the tutor will allow the participants to discuss freely, making sure that it does not get out of hand, and then come in at the end with any reinforcement or missed points.

A Typical Session

Julie, the company interpersonal skills trainer, is running a course on grievance handling. She has explained the knowledge of the company grievance procedure and discussed the judgement options of handling staff grievances, from outright acceptance to total rejection, with many shades in between. She has also demonstrated the skills of implementing some of these options. Bryan is now practising his skills of handling a grievance in a role play with Julie. The role play has Julie complaining to Bryan, her manager, that she is unable to take her company car with her on a touring holiday in France. (The company policy does not allow cars to be taken overseas as there is no insurance cover.) One of the skills Julie has demonstrated is how to project concern without commitment and how to avoid allowing the grievance to degenerate into an argument. This is what Bryan has been practising. Julie is about to help him let off steam and she will then give him feedback on his ability to implement his judgement.

Julie: Thanks Bryan, I rather like the idea of a holiday in France!

How do you feel the interview went?

Bryan: Not too bad, but I found it difficult to avoid being drawn into an argument.

Julie: Which particular instances are you thinking of?

Bryan: There was a bit when you implied that it was your car and that you could do what you liked with it. I was being drawn because I felt that you were forgetting that having a company car is a great privilege that lots of people really envy.

Julie: I actually said, 'The car is part of my salary package and is mine to do with as I want' and you replied, 'You're very lucky to have a car at all'.

Bryan: That's right.

Julie: When you said that, I felt that I had to justify myself and that this would lead to an argument. How do you think you might have avoided this from happening?

Bryan: I'm not sure. I am prone to having a short fuse when I think people are being unreasonable.

Julie: Perhaps you could use the 'reflecting' skill we've been looking at and repeat back to me what I am saying. This will show that you are listening and will give you thinking time.

Bryan: OK.

Julie: Shall we try it? 'The car is part of my salary package and is mine to do with as I want'.

Bryan: 'So you see it as your personal car.'

Julie: That made me feel that you were prepared to understand my point of view – though not necessarily agree with it. How comfortable did you feel saying it?

Bryan: Yes, it was fine.

Julie: I liked the way you asked me, 'How long have you been planning this holiday?' because it showed that you were concerned that I had been looking forward to it.

The conversation would continue along these lines highlighting what Bryan had done well and helping him with problem areas. Julie is an excellent trainer who has demonstrated the skills that Bryan is to learn. The well designed role play has enabled Bryan to practise and he has worked hard in practising those skills. Most of his feedback is, therefore, praise rather than criticism and the atmosphere is similar to a celebration. As the skills have been well defined, the role play has been kept focused and short and the other participants have not been kept quiet for very long. Had Julie been unable to remember some of the words used or had she wanted to give feedback on some of the body language, the role play had been video taped. As it was, she did not use the play back, but kept the camera on for the feedback session as well. At the end of the session she gave Bryan the tape with the feedback on so that he could use it for revision. All Bryan's subsequent practice sessions were recorded on to the same tape that he took away with him at the end of the programme.

A (Hopefully) Less Typical Session

Some students are not as eager to learn as Bryan and can be quite resistant to the feedback. (We shall discuss different thresholds to criticism in the next chapter.) In these circumstances, it is important that the tutor remains and gets the point across without browbeating the trainee or being intimidated in return. Tony was the such potentially difficult student when Roger began giving him feedback after a presentation skills practical session.

Roger: Well, Tony, how do you think that went?

Tony: Fine. No problems.

Roger: Is there anything you might do differently next time?

Tony: No.

Roger: Let's look at the introduction. What were you including in this?

Tony: I included everything I was supposed to, everything you told me to include. There was a title, an objective, an incentive to listen and an outline of the structure of the presentation.
What more can I say?

Roger: You said that your objective was, 'to talk about the company disciplinary procedures'. That –

Tony: Yes, that's right. That was the objective.

Roger: When we spoke about objectives this morning, I said that they should be 'learner-centred' in that the trainees, the listeners to your presentation, should know what they are expected to do with the information after your presentation. The way you stated the objective it was 'trainer-centred' – it described what *you* were going to do rather than what *they* were expected to do.

Tony: I think you're just splitting hairs. It means the same.

Roger: You don't see any real importance in describing the objectives in 'learner-centred' rather than 'trainer-centred' terms?

Tony: No. It's just playing with words.

Roger: The reason for the distinction is twofold. Firstly, it establishes that the presentation is for the benefit of the trainees rather than the trainer. Secondly, a 'learner-centred' objective gives a way of checking how much the students have actually learnt.

Tony: How should it be written then?

Roger: 'At the end of my presentation you will be able to describe the company disciplinary procedures, what levels of discipline can be administered by yourselves directly and which need reference to the personnel department.'

Tony: OK.

Tony has been told firmly about how objectives must be written for company presentations. Roger will monitor this on the next practice session and, hopefully, Tony will do it properly and attract praise. If he still does not conform, it is probably more an attitude problem than a difficulty with the mental skill of writing objectives. A 'will not' more than a 'cannot'. Roger will have to consider what action to take next. Chapter 9 on feedback, debriefing and reporting discusses some options.

EXERCISE

Watch a television version of Talent Time or Opportunity Knocks where amateur entertainers perform to try to break through into the 'big time'. At the end of the show, established performers will give their feedback on how the amateurs did and what they need to do to improve their act. Listen to how the feedback is being given and check it against the ten rules and the feedback formula. Then notice the faces of the recipients who have put months of work into their three-minute, once in a lifetime opportunity.

Review

We have discussed many of the issues involved in giving feedback: who should do it, how, when and where. The ten rules for giving feedback and the feedback formula are essential if the feedback is to be effective in helping the trainees to learn without upsetting the relationships between learners and trainers.

CHECKLIST FOR THE TRAINER

- **Does your feedback conform to the ten rules of giving feedback?**
- **Are your means of observation and recording (observation sheets, video and audio) specific and objective?**
- **How are you dealing with the participant who is practising?**
- **How are you dealing with the participants who are not practising?**
- **Are you following the feedback formula?**

---

5 How People Receive Feedback

  SUMMARY

This chapter:
- details people's different capacities for receiving feedback, lists how they indicate those capacities and produces a model for the acceptance of feedback;
- describes how to set a supportive climate for trainees to receive feedback;
- considers some cultural differences in how feedback is received;
- explains why and when trainees have received enough feedback and lists those signals that indicate that the feedback should end;
- suggests the most effective way for trainers to receive feedback.

While it is important to develop the skills and the strategies for giving feedback, it is equally necessary to consider what is going on inside the recipient's mind so that we can gauge how they are feeling and alter our plans accordingly.

People's Different Capacities for Receiving Feedback

People vary in the amount of criticism that they can take and an individual will even differ from day to day and from task to task. Before we begin giving feedback it would certainly be useful if we could estimate what the trainee's capacity is likely to be. Fortunately most people will tell us – if we only ask! We established earlier the advantages of asking the learner, who is to receive the feedback, to make the first comments about how they feel the exercise went. By listening carefully to the response we can gain a fair insight into how they are feeling at that moment and their capacity for feedback.

A Model for Accepting Criticism

It is as though inside each person there is a container that is used to collect the criticism they receive. Each time we criticize the trainee it is like putting liquid into a glass and, as the comments continue, we can hear the glass filling up. If the comment is accepted the trainee will respond with:

- 'Yes, I can see that now'
- 'That's helpful'
- 'Can you tell me more about that?'

As the level reaches the top of the glass we will hear the student hesitate:

- 'I think I can see what you mean'
- 'I'm not sure about that'
- 'Maybe yes, maybe no'.

The 'Thimble', the 'Tumbler' and the 'Bucket'

The glass will vary in size according to a number of factors. Typically, we carry around a *tumbler* that can take about three or four pieces of criticism. The *thimble* will only be able to take one or two, but the *bucket* will accept a very much greater number of points.

The *thimble* is the person who is not expecting, or is not wanting, to hear of many problem areas. When asked how they felt the session went, thimbles might reply:

- 'Pretty well'
- 'It was easier than I thought it would be'
- 'You tell me'.

If they were to receive more than one or two criticisms they would be surprised and, possibly, resistant.

The *tumbler* will take about three or four pieces of criticism, though this figure is only an average as it could be that the first comment touches them on a raw nerve and fills up their glass in one go. These three criticisms could be three different points or the same point made three times (which reinforces our warnings about using observers and video as means of feedback). When asked how the exercise went, tumblers will reply:

- 'Not too bad, but there were one or two things that I wasn't happy with'

– 'I started off all right, but I tended to lose it after a while'
– 'I wouldn't mind another go at that'.

The *bucket* is the person who appears to be able to take a great amount of criticism. Sometimes it is a *genuine bucket*, someone who is new to the skill, is self-assured and wants to learn as much as possible. Often it is *a bucket with a hole in*, where the criticisms go in through the top and come straight out through the bottom – without touching the sides. *The bucket with a hole in* seems highly receptive to feedback, but is probably as resistant as the thimble. The genuine bucket will make comments like:

– 'That was very difficult'
– 'I've got a lot to learn'
– 'I really messed that up'

The bucket with a hole in will make exaggerated comments:

– 'That was absolutely dreadful'
– 'I hope that no-one ever hears about this'
– 'I feel really embarrassed'

and will back these up with some predictable body language. As they carry out this self- criticism, they will ensure that they do not look at anybody, unlike the genuine buckets who will look at the trainer. The buckets with a hole in will look around the room, at the ceiling, the walls and the floor. Then, all of a sudden, they will stare at one of the 'people persons' in the room. The 'people person', who might be the trainer as much as it might be a fellow participant, will feel very uncomfortable in front of this self-flagellation. Out of embarrassment, the 'people person' will say:

– 'It wasn't that bad'
– 'I think you are being rather hard on yourself'
– 'No, really, it was quite good'.

At this point, the bucket with a hole in has won. It will now be extremely difficult for the trainer to come out with criticisms after the general consensus has been announced that the performance was good. If, having been asked how the session went, the trainees begin demonstrating that they are buckets with a hole in, it is essential that the tutor interrupts and asks the trainees which particular parts they found difficult. At this point, the buckets with a hole in will typically back pedal and the self-criticism will stop. If the trainer does not intervene, a pattern of 'mutual niceness' might develop where trainees make kind platitudes to each other as an investment for when it is their turn.

Being a thimble, a tumbler or a bucket can be due to several factors.

Certainly some people are born more sensitive to criticism than others. However, the environment has a part to play. The more vulnerable the trainees feel the more likely they are to represent a thimble. As they feel more supported, so the volume of the glass expands. The more we can implement the ideas on setting the supportive climate mentioned later in this chapter, the greater will be the capacity for feedback. If trainees are new to a skill, their vessel will be bigger than if they feel they should already have a certain level of competence. Their relationship with the trainer and the other learners will have an effect as will the previous comments they have made about having to do the exercise. Because of the situational factors, it is certainly possible for someone to be a thimble for one task but a bucket for another.

> Paul and Annie had different reactions when they knew they were to attend a training course on supervisory skills. As they were discussing the course with other participants, Annie said she was very keen because, being new to the job, she felt she had much to learn. Paul, on the other hand, was rather confused about why he had been selected. He told his colleagues that he had been a supervisor for four years and thought that he had picked up the essentials of the job already by trial and error. While he would have appreciated attending in the early days, he felt that now was a little too late. After their respective role play sessions, Paul represented a thimble, while Annie was more of a large tumbler.

Other Reactions

Occasionally, when asked to comment on their performance, trainees will report that their mind has gone blank and that they cannot remember anything about it. There are times when trainees will have a genuine short-term amnesia after the event, particularly if they have committed a great deal of emotional energy to the task. Equally, it is possible for the trainee to burst into tears of relief immediately the exercise is over. These actions can occur in thimbles as much as in buckets and do not reflect the size of the container.

Sometimes the trainee is reluctant to offer any sort of self-criticism and when asked how they felt their session went will respond with a simple, 'I don't know. You tell me.' This reaction is most common in thimbles. They either secretly think that they did well and want to hear it from the tutor rather than sound conceited or they feel it was not so good and do not want to add themselves to the potential critics. Whatever the reason, the trainer should press ahead with the feedback and listen and watch carefully for the defences.

Effects of Praise

If criticism has the effect of raising the level of liquid in the glass, praise has the effect of lowering it. However, the quantities involved are of a different order of magnitude. It is more appropriate to think of praise as being blotting paper, removing only small quantities of liquid at a time. It would be wrong to think that one unit of criticism can be removed by a single unit of praise; it will take much more than one piece of praise to achieve that. However, we are likely to be giving more praise than criticism anyway if we are aiming to reinforce positive behaviours.

There is a view of training that we should only ever catch people doing right and should make no comment if they make mistakes. The belief is that people are 'praise seeking' and will learn just through positive reinforcement. If an action is not rewarded, the trainee will find no incentive to reproduce it and will thus not do it again. In this way, mistakes are eliminated. Certainly, learners' performance does improve with praise, as shown in Figure 5.1.

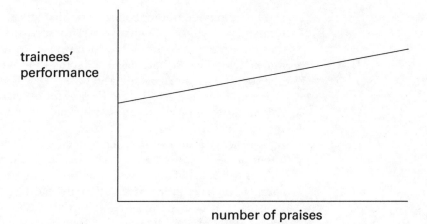

Figure 5.1 *How trainee performance changes with praise*

The rate of improvement, shown by the angle of the slope, is related to age and culture. Younger people and those from more praising cultures will show a greater improvement than older people and those from less praising cultures. For the latter, cynicism will creep in when they recognize that they are only receiving praise and they are likely to become suspicious of the trainer. For these people, interspersing a few criticisms seems to add to the value of the praise.

Leaving the 'Glass' Overnight

If a full glass of water is left overnight then the level will have gone down a little by the following morning, just through evaporation. The same happens with a glass full of criticism. The next day, the trainee can arrive with a fairly full container, not an empty one, and so the amount of criticism that can be taken may not be too great. This should not cause too much of a problem, however, as the trainee should be improving and so attract more praise.

If it is a different skill to be learned on another day, the learner will begin with a new, empty glass. However, the size of this new glass will be affected by the previous relationship that the trainee has had with the trainer and the environment and the trainee's previous contact with the skill.

Habituation and Sensitization

Habituation

Habituation is a natural phenomenon that affects all animals, including humans, and without which we could not survive on this earth. It appears that the number of stimuli to which we can be attentive at any time is limited and, once we have dismissed something as unimportant, we focus our attention in more meaningful ways.

For animals that are likely to be prey for other animals this is vital. An animal continuously receives information about its surroundings through its five senses: of sight, sound, touch, taste and smell. The first time it hears a new sound, the animal will freeze and pay complete attention as the sound might warn of danger. If nothing happens, the animal will relax. The second time the animal hears exactly the same sound it will pay a little less attention, then less each following time until, eventually, it ceases to pay conscious attention and habituates to the sound. If this process did not take place, rabbits in the fields would spend their entire lives frozen to the spot as the wind rustled the leaves.

Humans suffer this same condition, which explains why we can live near a busy road and, after a short while, not hear the traffic. We can drive the same route to work each day and suddenly find ourselves in the office, having habituated to the journey. This also explains why everyone else's home smells – and ours does not! Figure 5.2 show how habituation causes people to pay decreasing attention to the repetition of the same stimulus.

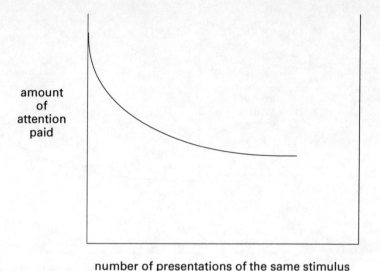

number of presentations of the same stimulus

Figure 5.2 *How habituation causes people to pay less attention*

Habituation has enormous implications for maintaining the attention of trainees during training sessions and is the reason why good trainers modulate their voice, switch to visual aids and include as much variation as they can.

Within a feedback session, it is possible that a receiver will habituate to the feedback and pay no attention. This is the equivalent of being nagged and leads to the content of the feedback being ignored. This will happen if the same criticism is being made in the same manner by the same person. The two ways to avoid habituation are to introduce new stimuli (or novelty) and to supply information which has a personal significance for the recipient. If the comments are made with novelty or the feedback is phrased in such a way as to have a personal significance to the recipient, habituation will not occur.

Sensitization

Sensitization is the opposite of habituation; it produces an increased level of attention rather than a decreased level. Sensitization happens infrequently, but what does cause it is when the stimulus is associated with extreme pain or extreme pleasure. In most cultures, we are not used to giving or receiving feedback that provides intense pleasure, so it is the

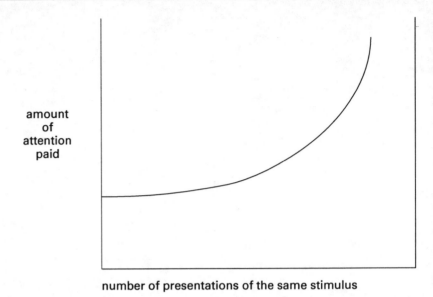

amount
of
attention
paid

number of presentations of the same stimulus

Figure 5.3 *How sensitization causes people to pay more attention*

pain effect that is more common. A certain phrase can be very painful and the more we hear it, the more attention we pay and the pain increases. 'If she says that one more time, I'm going to kill her!' would be a typical reaction. Thus, there is always the unfortunate possibility that the first time the trainer mentions a criticism, it is the final straw and the learner becomes sensitized to the comment; their glass will fill up in one go.

Figure 5.3 shows how sensitization causes people to pay increasing attention to the repetition of the same stimulus.

How to Set a Supportive Climate for Receiving Feedback

The amount of feedback that the trainees can take is directly related to how supported they feel during the training. If they feel that they will be humiliated or punished, they will be much more resistant to the feedback than if they know that the environment is conducive to learning and taking risks. Although the trainers might announce that it is to be a safe atmosphere, the behaviour of the instructors will carry more weight than the words. There are three occasions when the trainers should consider creating a supportive climate; these are given below, together with some tips on how the trainers might facilitate this.

Before the training takes place
- ensure that a thorough briefing is given to the trainees about why they are attending the training and what they will be expected to do on return
- try to encourage some contact between the trainees and the trainer to discuss what the training is about and any immediate concerns the trainee might have
- ensure that the trainees' domestic and work concerns are dealt with
- discuss the trainees' expectations of the training
- discuss what reports they have heard from previous participants
- ensure that comprehensive joining instructions are provided.

At the beginning of the training
- ensure that there is a welcoming reception for the trainees at the course venue, preferably meeting over coffee
- ensure that they are introduced to fellow trainees, if they do not already know them
- ensure that the trainers are introduced
- identify the trainees' hopes and any concerns about the training
- explain the structure of the course.

During the training
- maintain the open relationship between the trainees and the trainers
- involve the participants in decisions about the content of the training, where appropriate
- involve the participants in decisions about the process of the training, where appropriate.

Culture

In some more traditional cultures, children are raised to be modest more than honest and so, when asked to comment on their performance, they are quite likely, knowingly, to underestimate their ability. In this way they can sometimes disguise a true thimble as a tumbler. In more modern cultures, people are brought up to be more open and so will say more accurately how they feel. Some cultures find it difficult to accept praise in public and might actually deny the favourable comments they receive or attribute them to luck or to someone else. Despite this *apparent* rejection, the praise is as welcome to the individual as to people from more demonstrative backgrounds. In contrast, 'loss of face' is extremely important to some people where embarrassment at being criticized in front of peers can extend almost into shame. The need for group acceptance can be extremely powerful and there are times when students will deliberately perform poorly, or even fail, if they feel that to perform at their best would make them appear better than their colleagues and so risk rejection. Great sensitivity has to be shown when dealing with different cultures, especially if the feedback is to be given in public rather than in the confidence of just tutor to trainee.

Why and When Trainees Have Had Enough Feedback

Esteem

Esteem might be described as our perception of how others view us. We may not always be right in that perception, but esteem is whether we think others find us clever, witty, slow learners or good at football. We all have it, both trainers and trainees, and it determines how much criticism we are able to take in a given situation.

Initially, when the tutor gives trainees criticism the effect is to raise their esteem. The implication is that the trainer thinks that the trainees are important and wants them to improve and succeed. This is why trainees are grateful and receptive to the comments and their enhanced performance reflects this. As the criticism continues, however, the implication of this feedback shifts. Now the esteem of the trainees goes down as they feel that the trainer thinks of them as slow learners or inadequate. In front of an audience the trainee will feel even more vulnerable, which is why feedback in a group has to be handled more sensitively and be more restricted than in private.

When the trainees receive the first few comments, their energy goes into trying to improve. With children there is evidence to suggest that they try to do better mainly to please their teachers and their parents. In this way there exists a reciprocation of good feelings. The teacher raises the esteem of the children by showing a concern that the children improve and the pupils raise the esteem of the teacher by trying to do better and increase their results. For adults, the need to impress the tutor is not so high, though it can still exist.

As the criticism continues, however, the trainees' energy now moves to trying to prove that they are not slow learners or dim-witted. Figure 5.4 shows how the trainees' performance changes as they receive increasing amounts of criticism.

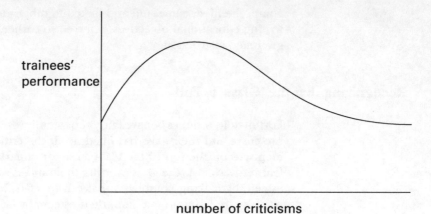

trainees'
performance

number of criticisms

Figure 5.4 *How trainee performance changes with criticism*

In the early stages of criticism, the rate of improvement is usually greater than the rate achieved through praise alone as shown in Figure 5.1.

The increasing criticism not only fails to improve performance, but actually has the effect of undoing the good work done earlier. It is crucial, therefore, for the trainer to identify when the top of the curve has been reached and to stop giving criticism beyond this point. Interestingly, after a period of extended criticism, the trainee's performance appears to increase slightly. This might be due to habituation as the criticism turns into nagging and the trainee becomes oblivious to it.

Operant Conditioning

B F Skinner (1953) carried out years of research into operant conditioning, looking at the effects of reward and punishment on the learning of skills. Although much of his work was related to animals, it found its way through to the teaching of humans. In the 1950s it emerged in the training method of programmed instruction and these days it is seen in computer-based and interactive video learning. The trainee is asked to perform a task or answer a question and the computer produces a reward or punishment according to whether the response was correct or not. The reward might be words of praise, an accumulating score or a cartoon character. It has been found with this type of learning that the rewards and punishments can have more impact than the lessons to be learnt. The learners can be become so excited trying to gain the next reward that they quickly forget what they learnt after that frame has passed. It is important, therefore, that summary tests are built in so the learning is

81

comprehended, cemented and linked to other ideas. Mager's books on writing educational objectives, referred to earlier, are examples of programmed instruction.

Recognizing that the 'Glass' is Full

Fortunately, trainees behave fairly consistently when they are at the top of the curve and their glass has filled up. If the criticism actually causes a meniscus on the top of the glass, hesitant remarks will be made as the learners waver. As the glass overfills, the trainees will try to preserve their esteem by making comments that can be classified into divisions. The trainees are trying to maintain their esteem by justifying the errors they made in their practice session. The excuses they make could well be valid, but the important issue is why the trainees feel a need to justify their position when they know that the criticisms are being made for their benefit. It can only be because they feel threatened and they feel the need to defend themselves. When this is the case, trainees usually go through three levels, or divisions, of defence, starting with division 1.

Division 1 Defences

In division 1, the trainees will justify themselves by attacking the environment they are in. They will try to find something about the situation that they can blame for their shortfall in performance. Typical division 1 defences will be:

- 'I'm not like that in real life'
- 'It's only a role play'
- 'I was very conscious of the video, the observers, the traffic, etc'.
- 'Someone had to go first, last, after lunch'
- 'I didn't have enough time to prepare'
- 'I thought about doing it that way'.

It is crucial how the trainers respond to these comments, though it is unlikely that they will need to stop the feedback after only one division 1 defence.

Division 2 Defences

If trainees feel even more pressurized, they will pull up their division 2 defences. Now they will try to defend themselves by attacking the person who put them in this uncomfortable position – namely the trainer! If the trainees are touched on a particularly raw nerve they will go straight to division 2, though usually it takes three or four attempts at division 1 before they drop to division 2. Typical division 2 defences are:

- 'That's all very well in theory'
- 'I told you I didn't want to do it'
- 'This exercise is stupid'
- 'I am only doing it the way you said'
- 'If you're so clever, you do it'

It is clearly harder for the trainer to handle division 2 defences from trainees as the trainers' own esteem is being brought into play and their credibility in front of the other trainees is being questioned. Obviously it is important that the trainer does not get drawn into an argument. Even if they were to win such an argument with the one trainee, they would quickly lose in front of the other learners who would close ranks.

Division 3 Defences

If division 2 defences are not well handled, ultimately the trainees are pushed into division 3. It is very rare for trainees to go straight into division 3 without going through at least one division 2 defence. In division 3, the trainees can only show 'fight or flight' responses or reactions.

The 'fight' is when they actually hit the trainer! This will be very unusual for any in-house training as the consequences for the trainees and their future employment with the company will be severely jeopardized. For a public training programme or college sessions, however, it is possible. A milder 'fight' can occur when the learner uses verbally, as opposed to non-verbally, aggressive behaviours. These might include threats and curses. The 'flight' is more common. The aim of the 'flight' is for the trainee to bring the criticisms to an end as quickly as possible or to avoid the comments altogether. The trainees might burst into tears, become extremely sullen or even rush out of the room. A frequent symptom is for the trainees' heads to go down as they appear to be engaging in copious note taking. This is an appeasement gesture that was learned to placate angry teachers and to prevent further punishment at school. Teachers never disturbed pupils who were taking notes as it looked as though they were keen learners. The trainee will also agree and nod vigorously in an attempt to encourage the trainer to speak faster and so end the agony quicker.

After Paul's role play, the trainer identified that Paul was probably a thimble and so he was careful to select the single most significant problem that Paul had and to provide feedback on that. He knew that Paul would be able to watch the performances of the other participants and to recognize mistakes in them that he had also made.

Annie was asked how she felt her appraisal interview practice had gone and remarked that she was fairly happy but she had had difficulties in confronting the appraisee with shortfalls in performance. She had also not found it easy to remain objective. The trainer agreed that these were her problems and began the feedback by discussing with Annie how to handle these areas. Being more of a tumbler she was keen to learn from these comments. Having covered these two points, the trainer listened carefully to Annie's response before deciding whether to introduce any more criticism. He did, of course, intersperse his feedback with several areas of praise where Annie did well.

Pre-emptive Defences

Sometimes the trainees feel so vulnerable that they come out with division 1, 2, or even a division 3 defence before they actually do the exercise:

– 'I can tell you, in advance, that I am going to make a mess of this as I am very conscious of the video and I didn't have much time to prepare'
– 'I really don't want to do this as the whole exercise is completely artificial'
– 'I'm only doing this because you're pressurizing me to'
– 'I flatly refuse!'

The trainer should make a mental note of these comments and listen intently to how the trainees give their initial assessment of their performance after the event. They can then judge whether the trainees are thimbles, tumblers or buckets.

A Warning

The division 1, 2 and 3 defences are natural reactions that trainees have when their esteem is taking a knock and they feel a need to defend themselves. It is very important for the trainer to be alert to these signals so that they know when to continue with the feedback and when to stop. Because of the significance of the signals, it is crucial that the trainers do not let the trainees know of their existence. If they did, the trainees might feel a division 1 coming on, know that it would be interpreted as a resistance to feedback and, very likely, suppress it for fear of being seen by the other trainees as over-sensitive. If the students did suppress a natural tendency to give division 1 or 2 defences, there is a real danger that they could be psychologically hurt.

How to deal with the defences that trainees use is covered in the next chapter.

How to Receive Feedback

During the course of the training, it is probable that the tutor will also be on the receiving end of feedback and, possibly, criticism from the trainees. As with the trainees, the trainer will also feel the tendency to go through division 1 and 2 defences, blaming the environment or even blaming the trainees for the difficulties that have been pointed out. In an attempt to justify the trainer's position, there is a danger that the esteem of the trainees might be lowered. The best way for the trainer to receive the criticism is to assume that it is being offered in good faith and is intended to be helpful. A simple formula for accepting the comments is:

1. Summarize the comments to check that they are understood.
2. Ask questions to clarify if necessary.
3. Accept the point and thank the contributor.

Occasionally, it is possible that the trainer may not agree with the criticism, but there is little point in arguing with the trainee. Instead, the tutor should accept and note the comment, so that, at a later time, it can be compared with the views of other participants.

EXERCISE

Watch a television question time programme where a panel of politicians is given feedback by members of the audience about government or opposition policies. Monitor how the panel member goes through division 1 and 2 defences. If you are lucky you might occasionally see a division 3!

Review

We have seen in this chapter how trainees receive feedback and how they reach and indicate their threshold. Criticism raises the liquid level in their 'glass' and praise lowers it. While we certainly do not have to fill each student's 'glass', it is important to recognize if it does become full and to try to prevent the trainee from moving beyond a division 1 defence.

CHECKLIST FOR THE TRAINER

- When asking the trainees to comment on their performance, are you identifying if they are thimbles, tumblers or buckets?
- Can you recognize when the trainees are giving division 1, division 2 or division 3 defences?
- Are you using praise to lower the level of the liquid?
- How are you setting up a supportive climate before, at the very beginning of and during the training?
- How are you adjusting your style for the different cultures of the trainees you may be instructing?

---

6 How to Turn Feedback into a Debrief

▷ SUMMARY ◁

This chapter:
- Defines the concept of debriefing;
- Describes how to deal with the defences that trainees use;
- Discusses the rationale behind the debrief;
- Explains how to turn feedback into debrief;
- Shows how to maintain the same review (feedback + debrief) time for each trainee;
- Suggests how to end the review

To identify the trainee's capacity for feedback and then to spot when the defences are being used is one thing. The skilled instructor must then be able to act quickly to prevent the student from receiving more criticism and yet not embarrass him or her by stopping the session abruptly.

The Concept of Debriefing

In any practice session, the trainee is likely to be developing a combination of knowledge, skills, judgement and, possibly, attitude. The review of performance will, therefore, cover aspects of all of these. The *feedback* will be appropriate for the areas where there is a right or a wrong, that is the knowledge and the skills. The *debrief* will be used in the other areas, where there is no right or wrong: the judgement. For attitude, many trainers will stick to the behavioural indications of the attitude. This means that they will give feedback on the knowledge or skills that seem to reflect a certain attitude. To make comments directly on an attitude is not easy as the

87

tutor will probably be interpreting behaviour and thus will not be able to keep to the third rule of feedback: that it should be objective.

The review will focus firstly on the feedback, advising the trainee about their knowledge and skills and then move to a debriefing of the judgements.

The Rationale Behind the Debrief

The reason for the defences mentioned in the previous chapter is that the trainees are feeling vulnerable. The worst action that the trainer can then take is to make it obvious that the feedback is being stopped because the trainee cannot take any more. 'I think we should stop the feedback now as we can all tell that Susan has had enough', will lower the trainee's esteem dramatically and move her into the division 3 'fight or flight'. It would not come across as genuine either, if the trainer immediately tried to identify something to praise. Although the trainee under the spotlight might not recognize the insincerity, the other trainees watching would and it would devalue the praise that they have received or will receive after their sessions. The integrity of the trainer would be quite rightly questioned and the supportive climate that they have worked so hard to create would be destroyed.

What has caused the vulnerability and the trainees' need for defences is the way that the feedback has been given:

- the focus has been on that individual trainee
- they have been exposed in front of an audience of their peer group
- it has been in an area of knowledge or skills where there is a right or wrong, and
- they have been told what they have done wrong.

The rationale behind the debrief is to move the trainees away from this situation in such a subtle way that it is not noticeable to them or the other trainees. The features of the debrief are that:

- the focus is moved away from the individual and on to the group
- the trainees who have been exposed are re-integrated into their peer group
- it is in an area of judgment where there is no right or wrong
- therefore, the trainees can no longer be told what they have done wrong.

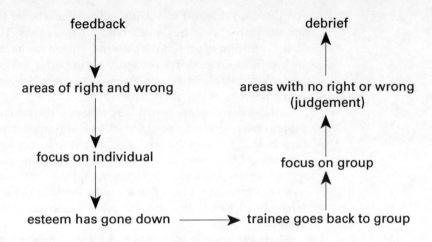

Figure 6.1 *How feedback is moved to debriefing*

When students receive excessive criticism, their esteem may go down and their tendency will be to look to their fellow students for support and gain the reassurance of being back in the group. The move from feedback to debrief facilitates this. For the feedback, the tutor's focus is on the individual who is under the spotlight; for the debrief, the focus is on the whole group's re-integration of that individual. This is illustrated in Figure 6.1.

This means that the review of performance is shifted from feedback on the knowledge and skills of the individual to a debrief on the judgement issues involved in the sessions.

How to Deal with the Defences that Trainees Use

The indication that the time might be right to move from feedback to debrief is when defences are spotted coming from the trainee. Trainees know that the training is for their benefit and that the feedback is intended to help them to learn. It is only by receiving feedback on performance that progress can be made and the learners want to make that progress. A supportive climate has been set to reduce the vulnerability and maintain esteem and the other participants are also going through the same practice sessions.

Despite this, trainees can still reach a stage when the criticism becomes excessive and they will feel that their esteem is being lowered. It is then that the learners will begin defending their actions. The defences are a natural reaction to protect the trainees' esteem from further damage and the justifications made for the shortfalls in performance are usually true; the participants really did not have much time to prepare or they actually were conscious of the video camera.

As these defences are real to the trainees and are an indication that the trainees have received enough feedback, it is important that the trainer does not argue with the defence. If the trainees say that they were conscious of the video camera then they were conscious of it and it only aggravates the situation if the trainer explains that other trainees forgot about the camera within a few seconds. Denying the trainees' division 1 defence will lower their esteem further and push them quickly into division 2.

When the trainer identifies a division 1 defence he or she should acknowledge what the student is saying, without necessarily agreeing or disagreeing with it. Clearly, this is even more important if the trainees use a division 2 defence, as agreeing will diminish the authority of the trainer and disagreeing will lead to an argument or even a division 3 defence.

Julian had just finished his first short practice session and had let off a little steam when Marie asked how he felt it went. He replied that it was not too bad; in fact he was quite pleased with the introduction, though he did find it hard to concentrate with an audience watching him. Judging Julian to be a 'thimble', Marie trod carefully. She asked him to talk more about the introduction so that she could reinforce where he felt comfortable. The major criticism that she wanted to cover was his eye contact, as he had not been looking at her during the role play but had allowed his eyes to stare at the carpet and this had the effect that she did not find it easy to talk to him. If she could improve just this one aspect of his skills from the first practice she would claim that it was worthwhile. Julian came back with the division 1 defence that he was too conscious of the other participants. Marie acknowledged, 'So you were distracted by the others?' Julian agreed. Without committing herself on the validity of his excuse, Marie indicated that she had heard him. She was not going to withdraw the criticism, however. Her feedback was still true. She briefly explained to Julian the importance of maintaining eye contact during an interview, which he accepted, and then moved into the debrief. For his next practice later that day, Marie would remind him about the eye contact and would almost certainly see an improvement. As the whole role play had only lasted two minutes, this was fairly cost-effective training.

How to Turn Feedback into a Debrief

How to shift the focus

Having identified that it is time to move into the debrief, the tutor will identify an area of judgement that was covered in the exercise, devise an open-ended question about that judgement and throw it open to the whole group, including the trainee who had been receiving the feedback, to discuss. At the same time, the trainer will slowly shift eye contact away from the original trainee on whom attention had been focused and round to the group.

Having judged that the time was right to move Julian's session into a debrief, Marie asked, 'I noticed that in this particular counselling interview, you did not take any notes. When might it be appropriate to take notes and what might be the disadvantages of doing so?

There are no right or wrong answers to this open-ended question, but it is one of the very relevant judgements that trainee counsellors should consider every time they counsel someone. One of the beauties of the English language is that the pronoun 'you' can be used in its singular sense when dealing with the individual trainee or used in its plural sense when discussing with a group. In this way, the trainer can begin the question by looking at the focused trainee, as though addressing them with the word 'you' in the singular, and then slowly, while asking the question, look around at the rest of the participants so that the question is finished with the implication that 'you' was in the plural.

Even if the session goes extremely well and there is little criticism to give, it is always good practice to turn the feedback into a debrief. The debrief would not then be protecting the trainee whose 'glass' may not have been very full. It would, however, maintain the pattern that all reviews end with a discussion where the other participants can be brought in. Trainees would notice if only those sessions that did not go well ended in a group discussion.

In the review session, it is certainly possible for the trainer to move from feedback to debrief and then back again to feedback, though this can present some difficulties. The trainee who has been practising might want to receive all the feedback while they are still under the spotlight. For the review to be directly on them, then not and then on again may make them feel that they are not receiving the full attention they deserve. The debrief will take the discussion away from the specific skills being practised and the focus of the session might be hard to bring back. It is also very difficult for the trainer to monitor the feelings of the trainee, when their attention is being dragged into the group. It is certainly much easier for the trainer to carry out the feedback with the individual trainee and then know that they have moved into the debrief with no intention of going back into feedback.

Designing the Debrief Question

The debrief question should be open-ended, where there is not a single answer but several views, and it should be related to the issues surrounding the exercise rather than to the knowledge or skills that the trainee was developing. For selection interviewing, for example, debrief questions might include:

- 'What is the effect of different seating positions on the tone of the interview?'
- 'How can we validate the references that the candidate supplies?'
- 'When, if at all, might stress interviewing be appropriate?'
- 'What are the differences between panel and individual interviewing?'

After a lengthy driving practice session, Pat asked Chris how he felt the session had gone. His reply suggested that he was a tumbler. He had known Pat for quite a few weeks by now and they had built up a rapport. There were no observers to the feedback session, but Chris had received several lessons by this stage. Pat gave him various detailed feedback on his steering, his braking and his clutch control. This included a mixture of praise and criticism, but at the fourth criticism she detected a division 1 defence as he blamed a pedestrian for distracting his attention. Pat acknowledged this, but at the second division 1 defence, she decided to move into the debrief. Without the benefit of other trainees to join the discussion, the judgement became a dialogue on what action they might consider if an emergency services vehicle was approaching from behind on a single-lane road, on a dual carriageway and in busy traffic.

The closer the debrief question is to the previous area of feedback, the less likely the participants will be to notice the change in direction and the easier the focused trainee will feel.

When the trainer has made a conscious decision that the trainee has received enough criticism it is important that the debrief question does not allow any opportunities for the other trainees to go back into feedback by commenting on what the spotlighted trainee did well or not. The trainer's first obligation has to be to the vulnerable trainee as it is the trainer who has put them in that position. The trainee is already feeling exposed and more criticism could be damaging. It is rare for the observing trainees to add more criticism out of malice. It is usually that they have had a new insight and, in their excitement at articulating it, they have become a little insensitive to the feelings of their colleague. The trainer should gently remind the other participants that they are discussing the more general question rather than a specific incident. If a few mild remarks fail to prevent the feedback, it may be necessary for the trainers to become firmer. They must protect the spotlighted trainee even if it means temporarily upsetting another learner. This upset can always be settled over the next tea break.

Maintaining the Same Review Times for Each Trainee

Apart from genuinely wanting to discuss the judgement issues surrounding a particular decision or application, the reason for moving into the debrief is so that the trainees do not realize that the feedback has finished and that the spotlighted learner has filled their 'glass'. To continue with the disguise, it is helpful if the length of each review is roughly the same for each learner after each practice session. The 'review time' is the sum of the time spent on the feedback and the time spent on the debrief.

For the thimble, the ratio of time spent will be much more on debrief than on feedback as only a few feedback points will be covered. For the genuine bucket, this ratio might be reversed as the trainee will be much more receptive to the feedback. For the typical tumbler, it might be about half and half.

The participants will not spot the shift from feedback to debrief and will therefore be unaware of how the trainer has interpreted the sensitivities of the trainees. From the participants' point of view, there has been equal discussion after each practice. Spending time reviewing trainees' practical work is rewarding for them as it recognizes the physical, mental and emotional efforts that they have put into preparation and delivery. Maintaining an equal length of review enables the rewards to be seen to be consistent and does not punish the thimble with a short review just because of their low threshold for criticism. Neither does it punish the trainee who did a near-perfect exercise because it was felt excessive praise might embarrass them or alienate them from their colleagues.

How to End the Review

At some point the trainers have to end the review of one trainee's performance and move on to the next practical session. A summary is always a good way of drawing together the learning points from a training session and the approach is just as applicable here – with one condition. The summary should only be of the points covered in the debrief, of the judgement issues. If there were to be any summary of the learning points of the individual trainee, this would constitute a repeat of the feedback and lead it into becoming excessive. The trainee would revert to a division 2 or even division 3 defence and the session would end on a very sour note. The debrief has integrated the spotlighted trainee back into the group. A summary of the feedback, be it by the trainers or the trainees themselves, would take them straight out of the group again.

> After Julian's role play, Marie summarized briefly the forms of note-taking that could be used in a counselling interview and the relative merits of these. She reminded the students of the dangers of note taking and how it might adversely affect the initial setting up of trust. Finally she thanked Julian for his effort, as it had raised many useful hints about counselling. She was sure that Georgina's next session would also bring out good learning tips.

Review

The debrief is an important part of the process of learning judgement in its own right. It has the added advantage that it can be used to phase out feedback and take the spotlight away from a vulnerable trainee. Maintaining the same review time of feedback and debrief combined, further disguises the rescuing of the learner and acts as an equal reward to the participants.

CHECKLIST FOR THE TRAINER

- Does every practice session enable judgements to be made as well as developing skills?
- Does every practice session have possible debrief questions planned in advance?

III
Debriefing

7 The Contexts for Debriefing

> ◁ SUMMARY ▷

This chapter considers the contexts for debriefing:
- on the job;
- off the job;
- after knowledge and skills sessions;
- during judgement and attitude sessions;
- the role play;
- the group or leadership exercise.

Debriefing skills are an essential part of every instructor's armoury and are to be used in a range of different situations. Before examining the actual skills of debriefing, we should consider where the skills are used.

On the Job

On-the-job instructors are likely to have been chosen because of their superior technical ability at the task and their years of proven experience. Being selected to be an on-the-job instructor can be seen as recognition for having achieved a high level of competence in the knowledge or skill. When on-the-job instructors, who are probably part-time at instructing and the rest of the time practitioners, become so familiar with their trade, it is not always easy for them to distinguish what is the prescribed company way to conduct an operation and what is just their preferred method. The distinction is important as it separates the knowledge and the skill from the judgement.

When Louise told Adam that you should always read the customer's name from their credit card and then refer to them by name, Adam was unsure whether this was just Louise's way or if it was company policy. When Sharon told Adam the following day that you should only refer to the customer's name from a credit card if you recognize them as regulars, Adam did not know who or what to believe and heard himself repeating what other trainee check-out assistants had said: 'But that's not what the other instructor told me!'

With seemingly conflicting information, trainees can become confused, lose confidence in their instructors or play one instructor off against another.

After an on-the-job training session, the instructors should be able to debrief the lesson, discuss with the trainees what happened in particular situations and what alternatives were available to them.

In some cases, the priorities of the business, safety or cost, demand that the on-the-job instructor takes over from the trainee to resolve a particular problem. After the crisis, the instructor can then debrief the occurrence by reviewing what happened and why the instructor took the action he or she did.

James was excited about the chance to land the aeroplane himself. Although he had many years' experience as a second officer and had landed aircraft in a simulator, this would be his first proper landing. Leonard had coached him well and had helped him to plan his descent. At 80 miles out, Leonard felt that James was leaving too many decisions to the last minute and would not be able to land safely. As commander of the flight, Leonard took control back from James and landed the 'plane himself. James had not done anything technically wrong and it was possible that he could have made a perfect landing. Leonard, understandably, did not want to take that risk.

It can often be helpful for the debriefing to take place in a relaxed environment over a coffee so that the trainees feel able to talk about some of the difficulties they have had and some of the factors they have considered in making decisions. The coach will be able to contribute related experiences that they have had which might broaden the trainees' options for future occasions, although the coach will remember that each incident is unique and what worked in one case will not necessarily work every time.

Off the Job

The pressures of off-the-job training are not usually as great as those on the job and more time is available to review options. The greater number of participants at an off-the-job session and the position of the instructor, being more central, often suggests a more structured relationship between the trainer and those being trained and a greater reliance on the instructor to have the answers. For knowledge and skill training this would be appropriate as there are answers and the trainer should be the person in the room most qualified to supply them. The trainer would use the various 'input' training techniques mentioned in Chapter 1. Perhaps they would use lectures or reading for the knowledge and demonstrations for the skills. For judgement training, however, the answers are not black and white and it is the shades of grey that are most important. The trainer's role is more to ask the relevant questions than to concentrate on the answers and the quality of the trainers is usually measured more by the questions they ask than the answers they supply.

Some trainees, particularly those who are a little insecure about their own ability to make decisions, will seek the approval of the instructor. This can create a dependence on the instructor which will either lead to inaction after the training or transference of that dependence on to the trainees' manager on return to their place of work. The manager is likely to think poorly of the training if the member of staff still asks what to do even after attending a training programme to learn what to do. At the beginning of the training programme, it will be necessary for the participants to have the confidence that the trainer is in control of the learning environment and this will necessarily engender a certain amount of dependence. However, it is important that the control is gradually released so that the learners have confidence in their own decisions and do not lose faith in the trainers who cannot provide ready solutions for every eventuality.

During a formal off-the-job training session, Gerry was asked for the company policy on charging airline passengers for carrying baggage in excess of their weight allowance, as shown on their ticket. He told the class that the guideline was that the first five kilograms above the allowance could be waived and the rest charged. As this was the official guideline, this constituted knowledge. Gerry was then asked if there could be times when the guideline was not followed. This became a debrief as Gerry was training the check-in staff in the judgement of using discretion and interpreting the guidelines. He asked the students the open-ended question, 'Under what circumstances might you not follow the guideline to the letter?'

After Knowledge and Skills Sessions

In Chapter 1 we discussed how learning can be broken into four components: knowledge, skills, judgement and attitude. Most learning is a combination of these, but demands different training techniques for each component. After sessions that look primarily at knowledge or skills, it is possible that some debriefing of judgements will come in.

After Knowledge Sessions

Feedback will be more common than debrief after knowledge sessions as the trainers confirm that the learners have the knowledge, which is right or wrong.

Where debrief will appear in such sessions is after the knowledge has been put across and the learners discuss the interpretation and application of that knowledge. Fewer jobs are now requiring staff to have just information. Technology is replacing that aspect of work. In supermarkets, check-out staff use bar scanning instead of remembering prices. Staff still need knowledge of rules and regulations to provide a foundation, but are increasingly being called upon to decide how to apply and adapt that knowledge. It is this aspect, the judgement, which requires debriefing.

'In Merton's Motors Ltd, the company policy on fighting in the workplace is that it could lead to summary dismissal.' That is knowledge and anyone who disagrees is wrong and would receive feedback accordingly. 'When Bill hit Henry on the head with a spanner and caused a fractured skull, Bill was dismissed'. That is also knowledge. If one mechanic swings a right hook at another and misses does that constitute fighting? How should the policy on fighting be interpreted? In these cases the knowledge is being developed into judgement and the feedback from the trainer would move into a debrief of the options of dealing with one or both mechanics and what information would need to be discovered before such decisions could be made.

After Skills Sessions

As with the debrief on the interpretation and application of knowledge after the foundations of knowledge have been laid, so with the debrief on the application of skills. The skills session will teach trainees the skill to the required standard. After the skills session, the debrief will enable the learners to decide when it is appropriate to use one skill and when to use another. These are the judgements of applying the skill.

Having learned the *physical skills* of accelerating and decelerating the car, when would it be appropriate to accelerate and when to decelerate?

Having learned the *mental skills* of fault-finding on a television set, when would it be appropriate to mend the fault and when to replace the whole component?

Having learned the *social skills* of refusing an unreasonable request, what constitutes an unreasonable request?

During Judgement and Attitude Sessions

Whereas debrief might occur *after* knowledge and skills sessions, it is an *integral part* of judgement and attitude sessions.

During Judgement Sessions

Debriefing really comes into its own during judgement sessions as it is here that the trainers will be exploring, with the learners, options for handling different situations. They are not brainstorming fanciful ideas in the hope that one might spark a practical solution, but considering deeply the implications of various courses of action.

During a training course for store managers, the participants are asked to decide what factors they would take into account and then what decision they would take, if any, in a situation where one staff member accused another of sexual harassment by following her to and from work each day.

During Attitude Sessions

Debriefing could well be used after an attitude session, though the motive would be slightly different. For an attitude-change training session to take place, it must be assumed that the actual attitude of the trainees does not match the desired attitude that it is deemed they should have. This does not necessarily cast any aspersion on the merits of these people. It could well be that the attitudes that were held were excellent for the job under the way it was conducted. Now, however, a decision has been made to change the operation and so staff will need new attitudes to conform to the new regime.

The Training Techniques Matrix (see Chapter 1) shows how this change of attitude might be effected with an input coming from various sources, but the process being group discussion and, particularly, group pressure. The intention of the debriefing is, therefore, less to look at options for ways of working than to develop ideas that will reinforce the new ways of thinking. It is the effect of the group and peer pressure in these discussions that carries the power that will ultimately be measured as commitment. Clearly, much planning and care has to go into such an operation or the group pressure might consolidate and conspire against the new ideas and just cement the old ones. The choice of who attends each session and an understanding of who influences whom and how this influence takes place is essential.

One form of input for attitude change listed in the Training Techniques Matrix is role reversal. Here the trainee is playing the role opposite to that which they would perform in real life, so a sales representative might play the part of a customer, a manager might play a union negotiator. The purpose is to enable the individual to experience what it feels like on the other side of the table. Clearly it would be pointless giving feedback on how they performed as they would not be in that position in real life. The debriefing would enable them to discuss the experience of being on the receiving end so that they would be in a better position to have more options when dealing with the real situation. They would be more attuned to how the other person feels and so, hopefully, come to decisions which take into account the needs and feelings of the other people.

A building society recognized the intense competition in the financial services sector and saw a great opportunity for selling additional services to existing customers who came into the branch. A training programme was designed to help the counter staff to appreciate their influence in creating or losing sales. On the programme, each participant was asked to visit a competitor's branch with a story about wanting to invest £10,000 from an inheritance. This the trainees did over an extended course lunch break. After lunch the trainer debriefed the exercise by asking the participants to relate their experiences, both good and bad. Having been in the role reversal of the customer rather than the counter staff, the participants were asked how they thought such a customer would have been treated in their own branch.

The Role Play

The purpose of role plays, apart from practising social skills, is to consider the potential consequences of different forms of action, to enable learners to experiment with different ideas and to see the possible outcomes. In this respect the role play is almost like a case study, but instead of the learners being external observers to the action, they become participants and the other learners can talk to the participants directly about what happened and what it felt like. The learners trying out their ideas are not practising specific skills, so it is not appropriate to give feedback on what they did right or wrong. They are considering possibilities in their decisions. Because there will be no feedback after this type of role play, there will be less need for sensitivity, so it is acceptable for other trainees to play both parts, rather than have the trainer take one as was recommended for the social skills role play. In this way, there can be several such exercises taking place concurrently, allowing plenty of opportunity for every participant to experiment. Of course, human beings are complex creatures and just because one person behaves in a certain way, there is no guarantee that everyone else will. It can be very instructive to allow different learners to experiment with different colleagues to learn how various people respond in seemingly similar situations.

A thorough debriefing of all the practical experiences will enable the learners to broaden their range of options when dealing with different people. Other role plays with demonstrations and practice will enable the participants to develop their skills and receive feedback.

The Group or Leadership Exercise

Such exercises are normally too complex and too long to provide any real basis for feedback. During a leadership exercise, the participant playing the part of the leader will have been using countless mental and social skills in handling the team members and making numerous decisions, both great and small. The exercise will have lasted anything from a few minutes to a few hours or even days. Given the individual's capacity for feedback, discussed in Chapter 5, it serves as an enormous injustice to restrict feedback to just a few random skills. Alternatively, to give feedback on every skill used would take several hours and drive the recipient over the brink! Multiply this one practical session by the number of participants who will have to endure the leadership exercises and the logistics of setting up such training become impossible.

Teamwork training is even worse. Every team member is the person using the skills and should be the recipient of feedback, whilst every other team member will be on the receiving end of everybody else's behaviour. The number of permutations and combinations of who is to give feedback to whom makes the whole exercise totally unworkable.

The only meaningful way to review the group exercise is to debrief it by asking the participants to consider what general points they have learned about planning, motivation, teamwork or whatever was the objective of the training session in the first place. It is essential to keep this debrief depersonalized to prevent feedback being given to any one participant.

Moreover, serious questions have to be asked about the whole validity of group exercises in training. They became a popular training technique in the 1960s and suffer from that anachronism. Most Western countries at the time were governed by political parties that espoused the principles of socialism and a more participative society. 'Consultation' became a watchword for many politicians, particularly when dealing with trades unions. Trainers picked up the same themes and used management exercises and 'games' that encouraged leaders to involve everyone and openly criticised those who left group members out. To suggest that this stemmed from government policies of full employment might be cynical, but is probably not far from the truth. In different eras, leaders would be praised for reducing staff levels!

Knowledge of human psychology in the 1960s was not very deep. Most experimental psychology had been conducted on animals whereas human psychology was largely theoretical and lacking in supportive scientific data. It was with genuine interest, therefore, that trainers set groups tasks to complete so that everyone could discuss afterwards what they had learnt about how groups behave. Although our present knowledge of human psychology is by no means excellent, so much work has been conducted on these tasks that there is enough evidence to predict fairly accurately how any group is likely to behave.

There was, however, a belief in the 1960s that has subsequently been shown to be fundamentally flawed and that really spells the death knell for the 'game'. The purpose of these exercises was to try to simulate in thirty minutes (or whatever was the duration of the task), the same lessons of group interaction that would occur in a participant's typical working environment. The belief held at the time was that the content of the task had no effect on how people worked on it. Subsequently, trainers could use deliberately irrelevant activities, such as building bridges and towers from children's bricks or completing jigsaws. After the exercise, the focus of attention would move to the process of interaction between the group members.

Unfortunately, the reality is that the content of an exercise is inextricably linked to the process of the participants. How people work together is a direct consequence of what they are working on. If the content has genuine results they will take it much more seriously than if it does not. Participants behave differently on the 'agree upon a three course lunch' exercise when they know that they really have to eat the food, than when they are told in advance they will not be eating it – especially if there is a vegetarian in the group! Clearly, therefore, to debrief an exercise which has an irrelevant content can only produce misleading information for trainees who think that all teams behave in the same way.

There are other factors which are also likely to confuse. Most training programmes comprise of participants from the same horizontal stratum of an organization. They are working in a group, therefore, with a leader whose authority is given by the tutor for a limited period of thirty minutes. After that time, the student will revert to the previous single status role. As the need to avoid rejection by the rest of the course is greater than the need to lead for thirty minutes, the leadership style that is most frequently used is very consultative and compromising. While this might have been appropriate for the participative 1960s, it may not always be in other times, when there is a real hierarchy and, perhaps, a more autocratic style of management.

Marshall McCluhan coined his famous aphorism, 'The Medium is the Message', when considering the impact of broadcast television on people's lives. Had he applied his slogan to training, he would have reached some interesting insights. If the medium of training is children's bricks, the message must be that leadership is child's play; if the medium is ranking assorted items when lost on the moon, the message must be that the company endorses managers making life and death decisions, from a position of total ignorance. Had McCluhan applied his view to outdoor exercises, he would have had a field day.

If trainers insist that course members complete all their activities and thinking in teams or syndicates, the message must be that all the best decisions are made in groups. No wonder that participants on time management courses complain that the single biggest waster of their time at work is attending too many meetings. They have been conditioned by their Training department to work in groups rather than to try to solve tasks individually!

Thus it is obvious that the only tasks that people should be working on are ones that are directly relevant to their jobs; those tasks must be extracted from their jobs. Now people can be debriefed on what they have learnt about the manner in which they work on the very tasks that they are employed to do. That is much more purposeful training.

Some group exercises are run with the expressed aim of trying to affect an attitude change. The published objective might be 'to enable participants to understand the problems caused by poor communication' or 'to understand the importance of working in groups'. Whilst there might be some legitimacy in these objectives for people who have no experience of working life, they would seem to be fairly pointless for staff who have worked in a company and experience the 'problems caused by poor communications' each day at work. The purpose of effective training should be to give people the knowledge, skills and judgements to communicate properly, not to set contrived exercises that attempt to reproduce everyday problems.

Review

Debriefing is an essential trainer skill and is applied through all areas of training where it is necessary for the learner to be able to decide how to interpret certain knowledge and apply certain skills rather than just stick to procedures. It also provides the learners with greater insights into how people might behave, leading to more flexibility and options.

CHECKLIST FOR THE TRAINER

- Can you distinguish what is your preferred method from what is company policy?
- How do you respond when asked for the 'answer' after a judgement session?
- How do you maintain your credibility if you are not giving the 'answer'?
- How do you help your trainees to tolerate the ambiguity of shades of grey?

---

8 How to Debrief a Session

	SUMMARY	
▷ SUMMARY ◁

This chapter:
- describes different styles of debriefing;
- considers the use of syndicates and reporters;
- considers the use of observers;
- explores the use of video in debriefing;
- suggests how to prevent more feedback being given;
- describes how to summarize the session.

Different Styles

In judgement training, as we have seen, there is no right or wrong answer to the areas being taught. It is entirely appropriate and consistent, therefore, that there is no right or wrong way to run judgement training sessions or debriefings. A range of possibilities exist from which we might consider just three: the central role, the participative role and the challenging role.

The Central Role

Here the trainers are clearly taking a dominant position. The debrief is structured through a series of open-ended questions, which are written on a flipchart or whiteboard. As responses are generated from among the participants, the trainers ask for explanations and views are written on the board. Only one trainee speaks at a time and all comments are channelled through the trainer who sits at the head of the table. This method is the easiest to run and is favoured by trainers and trainees who like structure in their training and who like to see what has been covered, as flipcharts of material can be displayed around the room.

To engineer this style of debrief, the trainer simply focuses attention, to the exclusion of everyone else, on the first person who answers the listed question, listening, nodding and asking for clarification. As the trainer stands to write the summarized contribution on the flipchart, the other participants will remain silent. On turning round, the next contributor will speak. The trainer repeats the process of focused attention and the pattern is set. Towards the end of the discussion, the trainers might add their own ideas if they feel that important points have been missed and yet would be of value to the learners. They do this in the same way as would the trainees, explaining the idea with examples, then summarizing and charting in a few succinct words. After exhaustion of the first debrief question, the trainer might introduce a second question. At the end of the whole debrief, the trainer would probably give a short summary of the issues that have come from the debrief.

Occasionally, because of the dominance of the trainer, participants are a little reluctant to speak and it can take some courage to talk first and break the silence. To pick on a learner by name can be embarrassing as that person might not have anything to say or may not be all that articulate. A technique which overcomes the difficulty is to ask participants to spend a couple of minutes writing down their personal ideas before reviewing these in the group. While this is happening, the trainers can watch who is writing and then ask that person by name what they have written down.

For most of the central style of debrief, the trainer will be standing up. As the trainer is taking such a dominant position, learners are most unlikely to interrupt or try to usurp authority. It is for this reason that instructors might decide to take the central role if they feel that the trainee who has been spotlighted is feeling vulnerable and might attract more criticism from the other participants.

It certainly can happen that two participants will see the same issue in completely different ways. This is one of the beauties of judgement and debriefing. With no right or wrong answer, it can be fascinating to investigate opposite perspectives.

After Karen's appraisal interview practice session, Marjorie moved the feedback into a debrief and opted for the central role. She sensed that there might be more criticism levelled at Karen by the other trainees. Karen had indicated earlier that she was probably a thimble and, therefore, would not feel happy receiving more feedback. The open question that Marjorie had prepared and had written on the flipchart was, 'Who should be consulted when preparing for someone's appraisal?' The debrief was predictably structured as learners suggested that the appraisee's manager and other department managers be brought in. When Charles ventured that the appraisee's subordinates be asked about their manager's ability, he put forward a well reasoned case and experience from his previous company. His fellow students were not impressed.

It would obviously not have been helpful for Marjorie to ask for a vote from everyone on their particular view. First, if such an agreement were to be forthcoming, it would be a knowledge not a judgement area, and there was no company policy on this. Second, it would have been likely that if most people viewed the point one way and only Charles viewed it the other, Charles would have felt isolated. With a contentious point like this in the central role style of debrief, all Marjorie had to do was simply write one of the views on the flipchart under the opening question and then pen a question mark next to it to indicate that the point was discussed and there were different ideas. It appeared on the chart as, 'Subordinates?' Honour was saved and, perhaps, a few options added to people's repertoire for appraisal interviewing.

The Participative Role

In this style, the trainers take a much less dominant role. They would initiate the debrief with an open question and then leave it to the participants to contribute as they want. There will not usually be a flipchart or whiteboard. There will be more cross-table discussion which will allow different perspectives on the same issue to be voiced. This could, in some cases, mean that the debrief becomes a little heated if controversial points are raised. The trainers will not be joining in the debrief, but will be noting both the content of what is being discussed and the process of how it is being discussed to ensure that no interpersonal problems arise and those who want to speak are able to do so. Should the debrief get a little out of hand or lose direction, the simple action of the trainer standing up and summarizing what has been discussed usually brings order. The discussion is then rekindled with another open-ended question. For most of the participative style of debrief, the trainers will be sitting down.

Kate had moved the feedback after Jeff's disciplinary interview role play into a debrief as she had detected a division 2 defence from him. Her debrief question was, 'When, if there is one, is the best time of day to carry out a disciplinary interview?' Nigel was adamant that it should be done first thing in the morning to allow plenty of time for the interview and to indicate to the staff member the importance of the meeting. Sheila was all for making it the last meeting of the day so that the 'offender' would not have the chance to go back to their colleagues to spread a possibly false account. They would also have overnight to calm down and reflect upon their actions and the punishment. 'So they can be miserable in their own time!', retorted Nigel.

While participants were considering constructively how the time of day might be a function of the timing and the gravity of the offence, Kate let the discussion run. When Nigel's comment risked 'light' being turned into 'heat', Kate stood up and summarized, 'So, the timing of a disciplinary interview depends on various factors.' Order returned to the group and Kate summarized the whole session.

To initiate the more participative role, the trainer acknowledges the first contribution made, by listening and asking for expansion, but instead of charting the point, the trainer looks towards other members of the group. As the trainer looks in certain directions, so people sitting in those areas around the table will be inclined to contribute. Bearing in mind the different learning styles, it is probably going to be the case that activists will be the most vocal and reflectors might say little, if anything. If some of the participants do not contribute during debrief sessions, there could be several reasons:

- they do not have anything new to add;
- they are reflecting on the other people's points;
- they are thinking about the next role play or practice session, which might be theirs;
- they have lost their concentration and do not want to risk contributing an idea that might already have been mentioned by someone else when their mind was elsewhere!

Before deciding to bring the quiet ones into the discussion, the trainer should decide what will be gained by it and what lost. If past experience has shown that the quiet person does make useful contributions when they say something, the decision might be to involve them. If bringing them in might lead to embarrassment or just repetition of someone else's point, it might be better to leave them out. To bring someone into the discussion, a simple glance in their direction might be sufficient. Alternatively, the tutor might mention their name and ask them a question in a way that raises their esteem by highlighting their individuality. 'Malcolm, from your experience of having worked in this country and abroad, what do you think?' is preferable to, 'What do you think, Malcolm?'

The Challenging Role

There might be times when the trainer wants to use a more challenging role for the debrief. This would be when it is important that the learners understand fully the implications of what they are suggesting because, after the training, they will be the ones who will have to carry out the ideas. To avoid dependence on the trainer, the trainees will be made to justify their views so that they have confidence in their own judgements. This is, obviously, the role that is most fraught with dangers. The participants must understand that the instructor is acting in their best interests in forcing them to support their case. The instructor will explain this in advance to them, reinforcing the purpose of the technique. To work effectively, the trainers and trainees must have established a very trusting and supportive relationship.

Sadly, there are some trainers who play the challenging role simply to ridicule their trainees. For the self-indulgent trainer this is very easy to do. The instructors know the role play or practice session very well; they probably wrote it. They have seen it run countless times and have heard hundreds of learners give their ideas during the debrief. The trainers will know every option that can come up and can rehearse counter-arguments. They also have control of the whole training operation and might even be reporting back to nominating managers.

To play the challenging role, the trainer will throw back an alternative view the contributors make their points. It is usually as well not to do this for the first two or three contributions or the rest of the group will fear opening their mouths. The counter-view put by the trainer must be depersonalized and not in any way be an attack on the trainee, only the content of what they are saying. The trainer will have to judge carefully who can be pushed and exactly how far. When the point has been explored or it is felt that the learner's enthusiasm for their own idea is dwindling, the trainers will back off. This does not mean that they back down or change their view. The trainer summarizes the arguments put forward and moves on. An occasional smile to the participants reminds them that the trainer's role is to challenge their thinking and this is not a game of one-upmanship.

As it is harder for the participants to discuss during a debrief of the challenging type, fewer of them will contribute. There will also be cases of side conversations where learners will check their point of view with a neighbour before venturing to risk it in the group. It is interesting to hear how the pronoun 'we' changes to 'I' as the trainee gains confidence from a side discussion to a plenary contribution!

> Keith was working with senior managers on a leadership programme. Linda had received feedback after her practice and the group was now in the debrief. Keith had previously explained that he would be using the challenging style as the participants would have to go back to their departments and implement some fairly major changes. The debrief was to review alternative ways of building the staff members into a team which was particularly necessary when people were faced with uncertain changes. Norman suggested a social evening for the staff and their families and explained that he had experienced such a system in his previous department and it had added to a sense of team spirit. Keith challenged, 'What about the person who doesn't want to socialize?' Norman agreed that some people were less sociable than others and might have other commitments outside work that would preclude them from attending. Sandra joined in: 'Something could be held in the lunch break', she volunteered. Keith came back, 'And who would pay for this?' Norman described how in his previous department, the manager had paid for half from some budget or other and the other half was paid for by the staff. 'How can a manager justify spending money on staff jamborees when there are people being made redundant in other parts of the company?', Keith asked.
>
> After another couple of exchanges, the debate was concluded with a summary from Keith about the pros and cons of social events for the staff as a means of team building.

The Use of Syndicates and Reporters

A popular way to conduct a debrief is to break a large group of learners into smaller groups or syndicates. A good size for a syndicate is around five people: they should have enough experiences to share and yet not feel inhibited by a large audience. It is rarely necessary for the trainers to ask the syndicates to appoint a leader, unless this role would provide relevant practice for someone who has received the input of a demonstration on how to lead a small group. The syndicate will be given a specific open-ended question to consider, a time period in which to consider it and instructions on what to do with the ideas that they generate. The quality of the debrief is of far greater importance than the ability to stick rigidly to a time limit and so over-running is not a problem unless it holds up other participants.

While the learners are in syndicate the trainers can take on various roles, again. These might include the central role, the participative role or the challenging role, though the trainer to trainee ratio rarely allows this luxury. It is most usual for the instructor to make an initial visit to each syndicate to check that they understand what they are supposed to be doing and then to make occasional entries to ensure progress and to monitor how syndicates are comparing on time.

After the syndicate debriefs, it is usual to bring back the groups for plenary presentations. This can be time-consuming and dreadfully dull for the syndicate members who are simply hearing their reporter relay what they know they have been discussing. For the other groups, they are hearing repetition of what happened in their group as well. The frustration caused by long syndicate reports can lead to disinterest by participants and even the occasional competitive or sarcastic remark.

To prevent these problems, it helps to ensure that each syndicate has been given a different question to answer. In this way, other syndicates will hear ideas different from those they generated themselves. The questions should be linked and follow on naturally from the feedback of the practice session. It is best to avoid questions viewed from the opposite stance as this might lead to a perception of competition which distracts learners from the real objectives of the sessions. Asking one syndicate to list the advantages while the other group lists the disadvantages can even lead to a count of the number of points and the team with the longer list declaring themselves superior.

It is not always necessary to have a reporter, unless this is a skill that is being developed by the training. The trainer can simply read through a flipchart produced by the syndicate and ask for examples. If the reporting skill is one of the objectives of the training, there must have been an input by the trainers and this would act as a model so that the reporters know what to report, how to report and how long to go on.

After the selection interview role play, Tony felt it would be a good idea to break the participants from a group of ten into two syndicates of five. He thought that it would break the pattern of the plenary debrief and also encourage some of the quieter participants to join in. One syndicate was asked to decide what information should be sent to external candidates before the interview. The other syndicate was asked to decide what information should be sent to internal candidates before the interview. Tony suggested that they produce a flipchart with bullet points on so that he could read these out when both syndicates returned and ask for expansion, where necessary.

When allocating participants into syndicates, the easiest split is purely random, with those people on the left going in one group, those at the back a second and the remainder, on the right hand side, being the third syndicate. It can sometimes be useful to be more deliberate in deciding the groups. Putting all the quiet ones in one team usually helps them to open up more, while keeping the high contributors together gradually reduces their volume! The decision might be made to spread the range of experiences and to have trainees work with people that they do not know well. Conversely, it might be best to keep together those who work closely so that they appreciate the relevance of each point and even produce action plans for implementation after the training. If the split into syndicates is not obviously random, trainees will ask, or certainly wonder, how the allocation has been made. To maintain the atmosphere of trust that has been built up, the trainers must be prepared to explain their decision.

The Use of Observers

As we have discussed, observers are not always reliable in what they observe, nor are they always skilled at giving feedback. Unless it has been explained to them, they will not appreciate the difference between feedback and debriefing. We should always be asking ourselves, therefore, whether we actually need observers.

Some commercially available training exercises specify that the task requires a certain number of participants. If that number does not tally with the number on the training programme, it is usual that one or two trainees will have to be left out. The role of observer is then seen to be that of an outsider and the quality of the observations sometimes reflects more a frustration and disappointment at not being involved than a true account of what was seen or heard. Rather than have learners left on the sidelines, it is better to use only those exercises where all the trainees can take part or where it does not matter how many people are in each syndicate.

Certainly, trainees can gain a great deal by watching other people carry out a task and then articulating what they have internalized. If this observation happens on a 'live' group the lessons will happen by accident, in that the observers will only learn from the incidents that they have seen occur. If an incident did not occur, the observers would not have seen it and could not have learned from the experience. Learning by accident is never the best form of learning. Rather than leave this learning to fate, it is better to have a prepared video of a team working on a task. The video can have been written to include all the points that it is felt are important so that there is learning by deliberation.

If observers are used, they should be issued with observation sheets; these sheets should all be different and the questions asked should require trainees to record actual incidents. Ideally, trainees should be discouraged from identifying the names of the exhibitors of the behaviours and, in this way, there can be no personalized feedback.

For the debriefing of a leadership exercise, the following might constitute one observation sheet looking specifically at how the task was done,

---

Observation Sheet 1 – The Task

What was the task?

What were the success criteria?

To what extent was the task achieved?

What was the strategy?

What was the plan?

What were the tactics?

What, if anything, caused deviations?

Other observation sheets might look at other aspects of the exercise, from how the team organized itself to the different types of role played by the participants.

The reason for the exercise is as an input on the judgement of how tasks are achieved and the debrief is to help learners who have limited experience to investigate the different possible processes that exist, so that they can speed up their experiences beyond the time that they would take in an ordinary, unstructured working life.

The Use of Video in Debriefing

Even more than when using video for feedback purposes, it is important that the camera is used simply to record what happened and to remind the participants. Some exercises can take a while to complete and during that time it is possible to forget an exact incident. The camera will always be panned back so as not to be focused on any one person who might then attract feedback. It is so easy for the self-indulgent trainer to record a trainee off-guard while that trainee is concentrating on an exercise. The playback usually does more to damage the trainer's credibility and relationships than it does to amuse the participants.

How to Prevent More Feedback

When trainers make the decision to move from feedback into debrief, it is either because all the feedback has been given or because they feel that the spotlighted trainees have reached their threshold and their glasses have filled up. It could be risky, therefore, to move back into feedback for fear that the trainee might fall into a division 3 defence: fight or flight. There are times, however, when such an interesting point comes up early in the feedback, that the trainers decide to consider those judgements then, rather than leave them until later. If the trainers review the session chronologically, it is likely that they are more interested in the sequence of judgements than in the performance of particular skills. When the trainers make an early move from feedback to debrief, the spotlighted trainee will have plenty of capacity left for more feedback and the trainers can return after the judgement point has been discussed. It is important to monitor the practising learner during this debrief, though, to see if they are happy to continue out of the focus or if they would sooner receive their feedback immediately. To move in and out of feedback and debriefing demands great concentration by the trainers and it is usually safer to feedback first and then debrief.

Once the trainers have decided that they want to finish the feedback on the rights and wrongs of specific knowledge and skills and move into a debrief of judgements, where there is no right or wrong, they will need to prevent other participants slipping back into feedback, as any further feedback might hurt the spotlighted trainee. The central role debriefing style usually inhibits such comments as the trainer is so much in control, asking open-ended debrief questions. For the less structured debrief styles, the risk is greater but can often be reduced by the trainers seating themselves next to the trainees who have been receiving the feedback. Should any negative comments be thrown at the learner, the trainers can simply lean across and protect them. The trainers can then explain to the accusing participants why certain action was taken and, if necessary, defend the main trainee. Once the practising learners recognize that they will be defended by the trainers there is less risk of a division 3 defence. This action will prevent the 'fight' being with another participant. The trainers will, obviously, have to be sensitive in how they defend the action of the spotlighted trainee so that it does not come across as condescending.

How to Summarize the Session

Depending upon the context of the debrief, it might last quite a long time and many good learning points might have been covered. A verbal summary by the trainers pulls together what has been learned in a couple of minutes and can crystallize and focus on the key issues. It is only the debrief that should be summarized and never the feedback to any trainee, which would make it excessive.

Some people revel in the freedom of an unstructured debrief in that it allows them to cover many subjects and to see links between other areas of learning. For the more pragmatic, though, there can sometimes be a lack of a conclusion or anything specific to read or act upon. It is not always possible to give a handout of the areas covered as the trainers may not have known at the outset the exact range. Recording on flipcharts can be very helpful as these can be typed up and distributed later. Whiteboards with built-in photocopiers make the distribution immediate. Alternatively the trainers can distribute notes of typical areas that have often been discussed during previous training, pointing out that this is not any official answer and there will be some points on the sheet that were not mentioned during the training and some ideas from the training that are not on the handouts.

Review

There are as many different contexts for running debrief sessions as there are styles for running them. In judgement there is no right or wrong answer. In judgement training there is no right or wrong way – only options.

CHECKLIST FOR TRAINERS

- Have you decided what role you are taking for the debrief?
- Have you organized your seating position to facilitate this role and to protect the spotlighted trainees?
- Have you organized your flipcharts or whiteboards to facilitate the role you are taking?
- Have you decided whether you want syndicates and observers and, if so, how these are to be chosen?
- Have you decided whether you will be using video?

IV
Reporting Back

9 Feedback, Debriefing and Reporting Back

▷   SUMMARY   ◁

This chapter:
- describes the advantages of not reporting back;
- contrasts these with the limitations;
- suggests what should be reported back and what should not;
- recommends how to report back.

So far we have considered feedback and debriefing within the closed environment of the training room. An important aspect of feedback is how far the comments are to be broadcast and whether or not reports are to be made available to the trainee's manager. There are certain advantages and disadvantages of doing this.

The Advantages of Not Reporting Back

Learning can be an enjoyable process to go through as we expand our minds and see new opportunities. However, it can also be difficult and stressful as we fear whether we will master these new skills or understand the information.

For experienced workers, to learn a new way of working might suggest that the previous, familiar methods were not the best and that for the past few years they have not been as good at the job as they thought they were. This can create feelings of insecurity.

For many of the older trainees, this training programme might be the first learning experience that they have had since leaving school and that might have been in less educationally enlightened times than now, when

123

teachers humiliated slow learners. Knowing that reports will not be sent back to their managers will help to alleviate some of their fears.

The reduction in pressure created by not having reports will assist the learners who think that they will take the longest to catch on. Fear of failure can inhibit learning, whether that fear is well founded or not.

For some, the fear of the training is amplified by their personal circumstances and their domestic situations, factors that would probably not be known to the trainers before the programme.

Mary was an excellent secretary and had qualifications in shorthand dictation and typing, though she had gained them quite a few years ago, before she had started a family. They were grown up now, of course, and had their own careers – Lucy was a marketing executive and James was in computers. Her husband, Stan, had worked for the Council since leaving school at the age of 15. 'A creature of habits' was how Mary described him. In the 30 years that she had known him he had developed his routine and he liked to stick to it. They rarely left their local town, had no need to really – their friends and family were there. They had never been abroad and the only nights they had spent apart were when Mary had given birth to Lucy in hospital. Mary had now been enrolled by her company on a three-day training course in London. She had never even been on a train by herself before, let alone stayed in an hotel.

Jerry had wanted to postpone attending the training, but that might have meant waiting another six months. Once he had the skills there was a greater chance of being promoted and, quite frankly, they needed the money. Starting a family was an expensive business; not only had his wife stopped working, but they had an extra mouth to feed and nappies and clothes to buy. Now he was leaving his wife and baby daughter only two days after the the birth. Would his wife be able to cope? How would the baby change while he was away? What if anything should happen? He would be able to telephone home each day, of course, but how much would that cost? And what would happen to his promotion chances if these worries became too much for him?

Advocates of confidentiality claim that the learners are already under enough pressure from the training and the circumstances, and that to add the stress of reports being sent to their managers would be too much.

Further, any report would be of performance influenced by the circumstances of the training and may not, therefore, be representative of true ability back at work. Equally, trainees would know that they were being observed and might perform in a way that was technically perfect, whereas on return to their normal environment they might revert to their old habits. Only if the learners feel that they are safe from reporting will they be able to discuss openly difficulties they have.

The Limitations of Not Reporting Back

Not everyone is as keen on not reporting back to managers on trainee performance. There are some compelling arguments *for* reporting.

Learning is an expensive process in terms of the time of the learners and trainers and the costs to the company. If participants know that there will be no report on their progress, some may not put in the extra effort required to overcome learning hurdles. Some people may not actually attend every lesson. They may avoid practice sessions and take a passive role in plenary ones.

It is certainly possible that not all trainees will achieve a total command of the skills to be learned within the short period of the formal training. Only by reporting back progress so far can the learner's manager know where to continue on-the-job coaching. It is true that the trainee can report the level of learning directly, but the trainer would be better qualified to describe how the learning might be continued. In some cases, learners might have a reason for not wanting to report back their progress.

> Bill was sent on the selection interviewing course because his company had decided to devolve many personnel activities to line managers and recruitment of staff was one of those activities. During the training, Bill showed that he could ask a range of different types of question, that he could listen accurately to the answers he was receiving and that he could control the flow of the interview. In role plays, however, he demonstrated racist, sexist and ageist attitudes that were not consistent with his organization's policies, and behaviours that could have landed the company and himself in court. When picked up on these by the instructor, Bill replied that he would recruit whomsoever he wanted. The trainer pointed out the company and legal positions and Bill said it was all socialist hogwash. On return from the course, Bill's manager asked

him how the course had gone and Bill grunted that it was alright. As the trainer had promised that no reports would be given to managers, only Bill and the trainer knew what would happen when he conducted his first interview.

In other situations, trainees might be very keen for the trainer to let their manager know how they got on.

Sue was delighted when the instructor confirmed that reports would be sent to her manager about the extent to which she had achieved the course objectives. 'I've worked really hard this week', she said, 'and I want my manager to know! When I get back, she'll ask how the course went and I don't want to sound as though I am blowing my own trumpet. I think it will sound much better if it comes from you. You can also help us to plan what further practice I need.'

It is now the trend to describe people's skills in terms of competence and a competence is the ability to do something to a specified level. Trainers should be providing certificates of competence at the end of training. A certificate of attendance might accurately show what has been taught but this might not truly reflect what has been learned. Whereas all trainees would be awarded attendance certificates, competence certificates would have to be earned and would show the commitment that the learner had put in. Certainly some people might fail to achieve that level, but that would just add to the worth of the paper for those who deserved one.

Within the United Kingdom and Australia, there is a move to enable workers to demonstrate their competence at work by helping them to assemble evidence of that competence which would lead to the award of a vocational qualification. A certificate of competence would carry more weight in their portfolio of prior learning experiences than a certificate of attendance.

When someone attends a training programme a contract is agreed in that the trainers agree to help the participants achieve the objectives of the learning and the nominating manager agrees to foot the bill. At the end of the programme, the trainer expects to be paid and should, therefore, in return, report the extent to which the objectives of the training have been met.

What Should and Should Not be Reported Back

There is a clear distinction between the trainees' performance of the objectives of the *content* of the training and their reaction and behaviour during the training *process*. Given the artificial setting of much training and the unknown personal circumstances of the trainees, it would seem inappropriate to comment on the trainees' level and quality of participation. For some people, it might be difficult to sit still for long periods of time and so they might fidget. Some learners will be very reflective and will come across as low contributors or even withdrawn. Others might be more activist, high contributors. These issues should not concern the learner's manager and should not be reported.

However, anything connected with the learner's achievement of the objectives should be recorded and reported so that there is a start point for further work and, in isolated cases, plans can be made to prevent the person from working in that area.

In rare situations, the trainee's behaviour on or outside the training may bring the reputation of the company or the training provider into disrepute and it would be necessary for this to reported to the trainee's manager and the trainee would probably be sent back early.

How to Report Back

The purpose of the training is to help the trainees to become more competent at the work for which they are employed or will be employed. The report should be a summary of the learning progress to date so that it can be assessed as to whether it is sufficient or whether more coaching is necessary.

While the achievement of the learning might attract a financial reward or even promotion, it is probably going to be the manager who makes that decision and not the trainer. The report is a snapshot of the learner's ability in an artificial setting and should not be relied upon as sole evidence of the trainee's ability to perform the job.

The report of end-of-training competence could well take the same form as that used to identify the individual's training needs in the first place.

It certainly helps if the information can be recorded in some observable way. This might be on audio or video tapes or, in the case of some physical skills, by the actual product of the skill. Alternatively, a written account will have to suffice. The more measurable the level of performance, the easier it is to plan improvement and to measure that those improvements have been attained. Further, it has the advantage of depersonalizing the report and so not threatening or criticizing the trainee.

Of the components: knowledge, skills, judgement and attitudes, knowledge is by far the easiest to learn, to test and to measure. Sadly, however, it is the also the least useful in most people's work as we are usually employed to use skills and judgement rather than just to know information. The staff member who can apply what they have learnt is worth more to the employer than the one who knows it in theory or can only regurgitate facts. Managers prefer reports on capabilities and these are likely to be more in the areas of skills and judgement.

The method of reporting should be related to the method of testing that is used to assess the level of the trainee's learning.

Reporting on a Trainee's Knowledge

One of the major problems with knowledge testing is that there is often a vast amount of information that it is felt necessary to learn to be able to perform a task. Testing and feedback on a random sample of information will be incomplete and may lead to false impressions; questions covering all the facts would be enormously time-consuming. To reduce this overload, the trainer has to be quite rigorous in deciding how the learner will subsequently use this new knowledge. If it is for *recall* purposes, the learner will have to be able to draw on these facts from memory without reference to any material. If the knowledge is to be used for *recognition* purposes, the trainee has merely to know that it has been covered and where to find the information. If the information being taught is neither going to be recalled nor recognized, it is highly likely that it will not be used at all. While it might be helpful as underpinning knowledge to help make decisions, it will probably not be such crucial information that the trainee must have it. It would, therefore, not feature in the report sent to the manager.

If the purpose of the report is to help the trainee and the manager to assess the extent to which the trainee has acquired the knowledge, it may be appropriate to award marks or give a percentage of the maximum score. If the purpose is to identify gaps in the knowledge, it is better to list the areas where the trainee has not acquired the correct information.

As there is so much knowledge associated with some jobs, it is useful to group it into those areas that must be known, those that should be known and those that it would be nice to know, as shown in Figure 9.1.

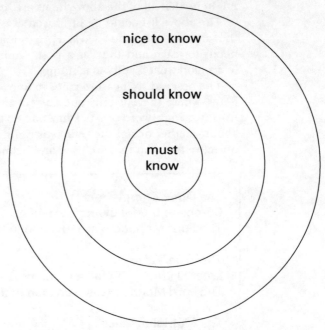

Figure 9.1 *Concentric circles of knowledge importance*

For example, for a new car salesperson, the knowledge they need might include, amongst many other things:

Must know	– price of the car
	– colours available
	– fuel it takes
	– how many miles to the gallon
	– different models available
	– servicing periods
Should know	– optional extras available
	– delivery times
	– insurance group
	– cost of a typical service
Nice to know	– painting procedure
	– how the car is made

The decision on which aspects of knowledge fall into each category depends upon the service that the sales manager wants to provide to the customers. For some dealerships, with very high standards, the policy might be that all of the above items are 'must knows'.

The above list could be produced as a checklist, in conjunction with the sales manager, and used as a pre-training measure of what the trainee needs to learn and then as a post-training measure of what has been learnt and what is still outstanding.

The best way to measure gains in knowledge is through objective test items, where there is only one correct answer to each question. This is usually a single word or a tick in a box, so that there can be no ambiguity about whether or not the trainee is right. There are four major types of objective test item that are used and below are examples of each.

The Open Completion
Complete the following sentence:
The Ford Mondeo was launched in the year . . . . ?

The True/False
Enter (T)true or (F) false in the box:
The Ford Mondeo was launched in the UK in the year 1992. ❏

The Multiple-choice
Tick the appropriate box
The Mondeo was launched in the UK in the year   1989 ❏
  1990 ❏
  1991 ❏
  1992 ❏
  1993 ❏

Matching
Match the following cars with the UK launch years by writing the appropriate letters in the boxes
A   Ford Sierra   ❏ 1975
B   Renault 25   ❏ 1980
C   Vauxhall Cavalier   ❏ 1984
D   Austin Metro   ❏ 1978
                   ❏ 1981

The answer to the open completion item is clearly and unambiguously, 1993. However, if the question had been:

'Complete the following sentence:
The Ford Mondeo was launched in the UK in . . . . ?',

the acceptable answers could include 'a blaze of glory' or 'a sense of expectation'!

The selection of which type of objective test item to use will depend upon whether the trainer is concerned with recall or recognition knowledge and the extent to which guesswork is allowed, as the true/false item has a 50 percent chance of being guessed correctly.

Objective test items are not easy to write and the interested reader is well advised to go further into this subject.

Measuring the trainees' performance and acquisition of knowledge by objective test items, be they written or verbal, by far outweighs other methods such as written essays where there is a greater tendency to be influenced by the trainees' writing and grammatical abilities, and their ability to bluff by using deliberately ambiguous phrases.

Objective test items can be written for each unit of knowledge, be it at a recognition or a recall level. The trainee would take the test and the results could either be used immediately as a means of feedback or later as the basis of the report.

Reporting on a Trainee's Skill

When reporting on the trainee's skill we must decide whether we are concerned with the product of what they produced by that skill, the process of how they achieved it, or both.

For *physical skills*, the product or the process might be significant and the method of monitoring performance will be by means of checklists. For the process checklist, the instructor will have to watch each trainee in turn to see the extent to which they conform to the procedures that are being taught. This is clearly time-consuming as the observation will have to be made sequentially, one trainee after another. For the product checklist, however, the instructor is concerned only with what the trainee has produced. The trainees can all work at the same time and call over the instructor when they have completed the task. Below are examples of checklists for process and product of the physical skill of changing a wheel on a car.

Process Checklist for the Physical Skill of Changing a Wheel on a Car

Did the trainee:

- Stop the car on hard level ground?
- Apply the handbrake sufficiently?
- Engage low gear?
- Put blocks in front of and behind wheels, in such a way as to prevent the car rolling?
- Remove tools and spare wheel?
- Check tyre pressure of spare wheel and adjust, if necessary?
- Place jack under chassis nearest to the wheel to be changed?
- Loosen wheel nuts?
- Jack up wheel approx. 2cm from ground?
- Remove nuts – top nut first?
- Remove wheel?
- Place spare wheel on hub?
- Put back the top nut first?
- Tighten all nuts diagonally?
- Lower jack – wheel on ground?
- Tighten nuts fully?
- Place spare wheel in carrier?

Product Checklist for the Physical Skill of Changing a Wheel on a Car

Does the wheel have:

- All the nuts replaced and fully tightened?
- The correct tyre pressure?
- The correct tread?
- The correct tyre size and configuration for the car?

Have the tools and spare tyre been replaced?

The instructor reporting on physical skills would apply the checklists and also objective standards of time and equipment used and can then give a report on the extent to which the trainees have achieved the standards and what needs to be done to improve, where necessary.

For *mental skills,* the observation of the mental processes that the learners use in the skill is much harder for the trainer to report on, as they are internal to the individuals and cannot be seen going on in their minds. The focus of the report is, therefore, much more on the product of the mental skill. For example, if we are training individuals to find faults in an electrical wiring system, we cannot see how they are analysing the situation, though we can tell if they find the right fault and how long it takes them.

By definition, skills are improved with practice and 'improving' means that the trainees are getting better. For them to get 'better' at the skill suggests that there must be an ultimate 'best'. For mental skills, this means that there is a right answer and the method of measuring the trainees' competence is whether or not they achieved that right answer. A mental skill might include numerical calculations for which there can be only one correct solution or fault-finding where the fault is correctly diagnosed or not. Giving objective evidence in these areas is relatively straightforward. The same methods of objective test items mentioned for knowledge testing can be applied to mental skills, as can a product checklist, as shown below.

Open Completion

Complete the following sum:
$47 + 63 + 83 = ?$

True/False

Enter (T) True or (F) False in the box:
If two trains are approaching each other at a 45° angle with one train travelling at 100 mph and the other at 80 mph, their collision speed would be 10 mph. ❑

Product Checklist for the Mental Skill of Calculating the Amount of Cloth Needed to Make a Suit of Clothes

Does the calculation:

- Accurately include all the customer's measurements?
- Include the prescribed allowance for pattern matching?
- Include the prescribed allowance for hems and stitching?
- Fit in with the width of the material available?
- Is it the same calculation as the trainer made!

Where speed, as well as accuracy, is part of the standard, a stopwatch can be used. In this way we can report that the student found three of the four faults within 20 minutes, without reference to design manuals.

For *social skills*, the focus of the social or interpersonal interaction is more on how the participants behaved than on the outcome of the interaction. The checklist approach is certainly applicable, but would need to concentrate on the feelings of the recipients of the behaviour of the trainees rather than on whether or not the procedure was followed. For example, when reporting on a trainee's ability to conduct a selection interview, a checklist on procedural knowledge might include the following:

Did the interviewer:

- Introduce him or herself by name?
- Check the name of the candidate?
- Offer the candidate refreshments?
- Enquire about the candidate's journey? etc.

Although these points could have been covered by the trainee interviewer, the manner in which they were covered could have been offensive. They would thus receive a positive report on a knowledge checklist, though their social skills were decidedly lacking. The social skills checklist would consider the quality with which the procedure was adhered to and perhaps ask the following:

Did the candidates feel:

- Put at ease?
- Able to talk?
- That they were welcomed?
- That they were just another candidate in a procession to be interviewed that morning?

If the trainer puts him or herself into the role play as the candidate, he or she can describe accurately how they felt and what it was the trainee did which caused this feeling. These observations would be included in the report.

Reporting on a Trainee's Judgement

By definition, the trainee's judgement cannot be right or wrong at the time that the judgement is made. Only with hindsight can the decision be evaluated. The decision can be deemed wrong at the time, but only if it ignores or mistakes some of the knowledge associated with the decision; company policies or laws, for example.

The report on the trainee's judgement can, therefore, only be whether or not the trainee has included all, or left out some of, the elements of the case that might have a bearing on the decision, and cannot be on the decision itself. To facilitate this, the trainer will discuss with the learner why they reached a certain conclusion and then use a 'factors of judgement' checklist to record which factors have been included. The interpretation of those factors, however, will be up to the trainee, as we discussed in Chapter 1.

The report on a trainee's ability at handling disciplinary interviews would include reports on knowledge, skills, judgement and attitude. These might include, among other aspects:

- The knowledge of employment laws and company procedures
- The mental skills of questioning, listening and summarizing
- The social skills of questioning and listening
- The judgement of the decision they made
- Their attitude towards the purpose of discipline

The 'factors of judgement' checklist for disciplining a late subordinate would include:

- How many times the subordinate had been late before
- Their years of service
- Their disciplinary record
- Their work record
- Whether they warned that they might be late
- Any personal or domestic problems that they have, etc.

If the trainee were given several such instances to tackle, it could be that they always omitted the question of personal problems. The report to the manager might then say:

> 'In each of the disciplinary situations handled, the trainee omitted to consider how the personal circumstances of the staff member might affect their behaviour.'

Reporting a Trainee's Attitudes

As attitudes are so difficult to define, it is easier for trainers to remain in the behavioural realms of knowledge, skills and judgement when reporting on a trainee. It might even be libellous if it was considered that some

135

of the attitudes were wrong. So, it is safer all round to report that 'Bill expressed a view that he would not conform to the Personnel procedures of recruitment and that he would select whomsoever he wanted' rather than 'Bill is an out-and-out racist.' Equally, when reporting on positive attitudes, it is not very helpful to say that 'Sue has a caring attitude towards customers.' It is more useful to her manager to be told that 'She can demonstrate, through her listening skills, that she can understand the needs of the customer.'

There should never be any surprises for the trainees about the report that is sent to their manager. The purpose of the report is to help the individuals to improve and develop, and this would be impossible if they were not told of the report. Not only can the learners not improve if they are not told where and how to, but it also sets the wrong tone if this communication is not open. The first discussion should be between the trainer and the learner as continual feedback during the training and this would culminate in an end-of-course training summary. Once agreed, the summary would be presented to the manager, preferably with the attendance of the instructor. Where this is not feasible, the trainer should always be available by telephone, if not in person, to amplify points and to guide on further development.

Review

Reporting on training courses has always been a thorny issue, with some trainers taking extremely strong views on either side. In this chapter we have considered the factors and how the reports might be made. The final decision on reporting will rest with the individual trainers and their relationship with the trainees and those who commission the training.

CHECKLIST FOR THE TRAINER

- Have you decided your views on reporting?
- Have you determined the views of the trainees and the commissioning manager?
- Is your company running a scheme enabling staff to accumulate credits towards an award of a vocational qualification?
- What particularly are you going to report back?
- How are you going to report it?

---

10 Feedback and Development Centres

▷   **SUMMARY**   ◁

This chapter:
- defines what a development centre is;
- describes the reasons for development centres;
- compares the different philosophical bases they may have;
- discusses the formats that development centres can take;
- describes the sources of feedback;
- suggests how the feedback might be handled.

The Human Resources function is increasingly blurring the old divides of Personnel and Training, and professional trainers are now less likely to confine their time just to the training of staff. Their role is to maximise the output of the entire human resources of the enterprise. In the same way that engineers are employed to maximise the output of the machinery, and accountants the return on the financial resources, so trainers are engaged to gain the greatest return on the investment in people.

This means that trainers not only advise on the identification and meeting of training needs, they also take stock of the human resources that are employed and plan how those resources can best be developed. This area of feedback is one of the most sensitive for trainers as the recipient's entire career and job future is being discussed. The emotional involvement is very high: decisions made here could affect the rest of a person's life.

Training v Development v Potential

It is important to clarify the distinction between training, development and potential before the concept of a development centre can be defined.

Training

Training is concerned only with an individual's current job. In that job is a desired performance – what that staff member is employed to do – which should bear similarities to the job description or the list of tasks and accountabilities. It should also be linked with the objectives for that person, which are used as an integral part of their performance appraisal. Although we might know the person's desired performance, it is possible that it is not the same as their actual performance. In other words, they may not be performing at the level for which they are being employed. Any deficiency might be due to a lack of knowledge, skills, judgements or attitudes, and so might be a training need. It might be caused by other factors, such as equipment, raw materials, pricing strategies or even the weather. In these cases it is not a training need. At least, it is not a training need of the individual we are reviewing, though it might be a training need of their superviser, buyers, maintenance colleagues or other personnel within the company. The equation for this can be seen as:

desired performance – actual performance = training
or non-training need.

From the equation, it is obvious that if we do not know a person's desired or actual performance in their current job, we cannot diagnose a training need.

Training consultants will know that a frequent cause of the actual performance being different from the desired performance is the organization's own unofficial, internal reward system. Companies can be extremely efficient at rewarding bad behaviour and punishing good behaviour. It is not uncommon for the person who comes up with a good idea at a meeting to be the one nominated to research it further. The staff who have no good ideas can leave work early. It does not take long before people learn not to be too enthusiastic!

Regardless of the causes, a training need is a deficiency in current performance and so must be dealt with as soon as possible or, cumulatively, the whole enterprise will fail to reach its objectives. Training is, therefore, remedial, mandatory and for the 'poor' performers.

Development

Development is about a person's next job. The equation of:

desired performance – actual performance = development or
non-development need

still holds good, but here we are predicting what a person's desired performance will be in the next few months, or years, or whatever time frame we are considering for development. We are trying to anticipate what their actual performance will be if there is no formal intervention.

In the old days, the 'next job' would almost certainly mean a promotion. With flatter organizational structures now, the 'next job' is more likely to be a lateral move. In businesses that are moving fast with technological changes or even just procedural changes, the 'next job' is probably not even a change in job title at all. The individual will retain the same job, but it will be conducted in a different way.

Development, then, means preparing the person with the knowledge, skills, judgements and attitudes that they will need in the future. There could be, of course, non-development solutions in the form of restructuring or even redundancy. Exactly as with the training need equation, so with the development need equation. We cannot diagnose a development need until we know what a person's desired performance will be and what their actual performance is likely to be.

Potential

Potential means that the person has the probable capability of performing in their next job, whatever that next job might be. Clearly, to say that a person 'has potential' is an incomplete and meaningless statement until we add to it what they have potential for or what their next job will be. Usually potential refers to the projected capacity to take on a more senior role or one with greater responsibilities, though it would be just as accurate to say that someone has potential for early retirement!

The Development Centre

The popularity of development centres is a result of the eventual realization that performance in a person's current job is not an accurate way of predicting how they will perform in a different job. For too many years, companies have promoted their best operator and then wondered why they have gained a bad manager. It is almost an inverse relationship that good sales staff become good sales managers. The qualities and competences of someone who is good at setting up short term relationships with customers and seeing the immediate result of their actions are quite different from those of the sales manager, who should be setting up long term relationships with colleagues and may not see any results for several months. To use promotion as a reward is clearly a risk. Being a manager should not be seen as a better job than being a clerk – it is just a different job which demands different abilities.

A development centre is an opportunity to identify what the actual attributes of an employee are, to discover that person's career aspirations and, possibly, to match these with existing or anticipated vacancies in the business. The development centre is unlikely to be a physical place. Although it might take place in the company's own training facilities, usually it is held offsite, away from day to day pressures and interruptions, perhaps at an hotel for an overnight stay. The sessions rarely last less than a whole day and may continue for several. The number of participants is kept low, often no more than a handful, and there might be as many observers and assessors. The assessors could be professional psychologists or well trained observers from Human Resources or a line function.

The approach is to measure the candidate from as many different angles as possible, through personality and psychometric questionnaires, to performance in exercises and role plays as well as group and individual interviews. Previous assessments and past records and appraisals will also be included. At the end of the centre it is usual to give feedback to the candidate on what was observed and the interpretations made. The feedback is usually a 'no holds barred', honest assessment of the person's strengths and weaknesses, where their career might go and what areas of development are needed for the person to achieve their aims.

The Reasons for Development Centres

There are several reasons why companies might want to conduct development centres.

The initiative might come directly from staff who want to discuss their career ambitions and to see how they fit in with the organization's long term plans. Most development centres rely upon voluntary self nominations, and this creates a very sound and open relationship between employers and employees.

Companies might be trying fill a particular vacancy that has arisen. A more thorough examination of the internal candidate could be an appropriate method to replace interviewing, as the cost of a wrong appointment can be so great. In such cases it is usual to use an assessment centre, the equivalent system for external applicants, if an internal appointment cannot be made.

Organizations might be undergoing an internal change or be participating in a takeover or merger. Thus, they will reviewing what human resources exist and how these might best be fitted to the new structure. This might involve people actually 're-applying for their own jobs'. It is a belief held by some people that when reorganization takes place, staff will be more committed to the new structure if they are successful in being reappointed. For those who are not successful, redundancy is often the prognosis.

As the world of work is changing so fast, enterprises occasionally like to take stock of what resources exist within their staff so that they can develop them singularly, or *en masse*, for the direction that the business is taking. This can be seen as an audit of the skills of the personnel employed.

The Different Philosophical Bases for Development Centres

The design of the development centre hides some fundamental beliefs about how an organization sees the attributes of its staff. These can be seen by the company's definition of competences and by the distinction between personality, attitude and behaviour.

Competences

It is very common for Human Resources professionals to talk about the competences of staff. The competence is an ability that the employee has that can be measured. As such the competence can be used neatly with the development need equation, which would be written as:

desired competences – actual competences = development needs.

All jobs within the organization can be broken down into the desired competences required to do that job, meaning that individuals can be assessed against each competence. A current deficiency in some of the competences would indicate training needs, while a difference between the competences required for a next job and the current competences which the individual displays, would reveal development needs.

The competences movement has taken such a stronghold that, in many countries, nationally recognized qualifications have been drawn up

141

to define the required competences required to conduct a particular occupation or profession. Measurement criteria have been established for each competence, so that a person can be recognized as competent and receive a certificate, or gain advice on what they need to do to become competent.

The Difficulty with Competences

The difficulty with competences is not the concept itself, but how they are defined – whether they are 'input' competences or 'output' competences.

The input competence is a particular ability of the employee and is what that person uses when they conduct their work. Input competences might include creativity, flexibility or commercial acumen. Output competences, in comparison, are what the individual actually does and what can be seen by an external observer. These might include being able to conduct a meeting, negotiate a deal or use a hammer. An individual's input competence does not guarantee that they possess the output competence, nor does having the output competence always mean that someone has the input competence.

The implications and complications of the difference between input and output competences can be seen through an analysis of personality, attitudes and behaviour. If development centres are designed to identify what people need to learn to prepare them for future jobs, the competences must comprise what people can learn. If they are to meet the previous classification made in Chapter 1, competences must be able to be divided into knowledge, skill, judgement and, possibly, attitudes. If the centre only identifies competence deficiencies in areas where the individual cannot learn, it can only serve to blight that person's development opportunities or focus them in another direction.

Personality v Attitudes v Behaviour

Different schools of thought exist about the role of personality, attitudes and behaviour; some individuals favour one above the others, while other individuals question the existence of the first two at all.

Personality

Personality can be described as 'a set of more or less stable factors, internal to a person, that make one person's behaviour consistent from one time to another, and different from the behaviour other people would manifest in comparable situations'. So, in greater detail, if these factors are 'more or less stable' then they are not going to change or, if they do, they will change only minimally. If the staff member's personality were to change significantly, that would imply that that person was unstable and would probably be unable to hold down the job.

Furthermore, if the personality is 'internal' then it cannot be observed and certainly cannot be measured.

The 'nature/nurture' argument among psychologists has raged for many years. Broadly, the debate centres around whether we inherit our personalities entirely from our parents, whether they develop in our early formative years, or if they derive from some combination of genetic input and environmental learning. Whatever the true ratio, most psychologists would agree that our personality is formed well before we start our working lives.

If an organization uses competences that are input rather than output based, a decision would have to be made as to how close these input competences are to personality traits. For example, if integrity is a personality trait, the level of integrity that a person has is now fixed and will not be expanded by development. Other examples of personality traits might include whether we are extravert or introvert, whether we are highly strung or unemotional, and our various forms of intelligence.

Human Resources departments that do believe strongly in personality determinants, invest heavily in personality testing at the recruitment stage and in development centres. However, although knowing someone's personality might well be predictive of their future behaviour, it would not enable any change to take place in their development, because their personality would not change. Similarly, input competences that are also personality traits could be identified at a development centre, but could not be developed.

Attitudes

Attitudes can be defined as 'an enduring system of positive or negative evaluations, feelings and tendencies toward action with respect to a social object'.

They are our beliefs – like a personal rule book or code of conduct – about how we feel towards a person, an object or an idea; attitudes include our various prejudices and biases. They are internal to us and so, like personality, cannot be seen or heard, but they drive our behaviours so that there is a reason for what we do rather than just acting randomly. Examples of attitudes might be that Manchester United are the best football team in the world, that smoking should be banned in public places and that television is responsible for any increase in domestic violence. There is probably a link between our attitudes and our personality though the effect of the environment on our attitudes is certainly greater.

If attitudes do exist it is likely that they are similar to the layers of an onion. Some will be so embedded as to be almost as strongly fortified as personality traits. To attempt to change them will either be ineffective, or so traumatic for the individual, that to try to do so would stretch the ethics of your relationship with them beyond reasonable limits. Unfortunately, although superficial attitudes can be changed easily, they can be changed back again with equal ease if they are not constantly reinforced.

Organizations that are more concerned about attitudes will conduct attitude questionnaires and surveys to determine candidates' beliefs and their preferred styles in handling customers, colleagues or teams. They may categorise these attitudes as input competences, although there is no guarantee that the preferred attitudes always produce the desired behaviour. It is unlikely, but someone's attitude may be that they believe customers are important but they are incapable of dealing with customers effectively. Some companies abound with enthusiastic, but incompetent amateurs!

A development centre might be able to identify candidates' attitudes and, if these are not too deep rooted, might be able to change some of them. If input competences are in the form of attitudes, some of these might be developed if it is found that the actual attitudes of the individual are different from the desired attitudes.

Behaviours

Behaviours are what people are seen or heard to be doing. They are the outward manifestations of our attitudes and can be identified by other people using their five senses. Behaviours can also be measured. Examples of behaviours might include wearing a Manchester United football shirt, scowling at people who smoke in public and hitting the television set.

If we refer to the learning classification outlined in Chapter 1, it is possible to see that knowledge, skills and judgements are all behaviours. Attitudes and personality, by this definition, are not. Human Resources specialists who prefer behaviours, concentrate more on output competences and put little time or energy into personality or attitude testing. They would expand the development needs equation as follows:

desired behaviour	–	actual behaviour	=	development needs
(for next job)		(in current job)		(to do next job)
K_D	–	K_A	=	K_T
S_D	–	S_A	=	S_T
J_D	–	J_A	=	J_T

(Where K is knowledge, S is skills and J is judgement. The subscripts $_D$ is for desired, $_A$ is for actual and $_T$ is for development.)

In this way they are ignoring, or paying little regard to, attitudes. Their justification would be that attitudes, even if they do exist, are extremely difficult to measure and even harder to change.

The development centre run by the behaviourists would define what output competences are needed for the next job and subtract from these the existing output competences of the candidates. This would then produce the development needs of that candidate for the next job.

The links between personality, attitudes and behaviour

Those people who do see a link between personality, attitudes and behaviour would normally describe it as shown in Figure 10.1.

An example might be that a person who has:

- a personality trait of introversion produces:
- an attitude towards parties that they are boring or stressful leading to:
- behaviours of declining invitations or leaving early.

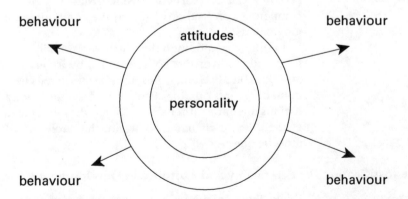

Figure 10.1 *The link between personality, attitudes and behaviour*

If you need to have people who are good at parties, these analysts would claim, it is best to recruit staff who have extravert personalities, who would probably, therefore, have positive attitudes towards the parties and would behave in the desired way of socializing.

In comparison, some people, the pure behaviourists, take an opposite view to the whole question of personalities and attitudes. They deny that personality and attitudes exist at all. They claim that at birth babies are like a blank sheet of paper on which their early experiences are written, and subsequently rewarded and punished. Over time these conditioned responses are generalised to take in similar situations. Attitudes do not exist; therefore, they are just a collection or pattern of rewarded or punished reactions to different stimuli. Equally, personality traits are just words that are used, like an envelope, to group together related behaviours.

There could be some sympathy for this absolutist view, as the only measurement technique for personality and attitudes is by the completion of questionnaires, either by the subjects themselves or by others who know them well. Answering questions is, by definition, a behaviour. Therefore, the collection of the results from the psychometric tests is nothing more than a grouping of behaviours – indeed, most personality tests are devised by factor analysis of different descriptions of people's behaviours. An interesting philosophical question is, 'Can a personality trait exist unless there is a word in the language for that trait?'

If an input competence, such as commercial acumen, is a personality factor, it cannot be changed. If it is an attitude, it might be possible to change it if it is not too embedded, but in that case it can easily be changed back again. If commercial acumen is a behaviour then it certainly can be learned provided that it is recognized as an output competence and subdivided into the component knowledge, skills and judgements.

In summary, although the words, 'personality' and 'attitudes' are used frequently in everyday conversations, their very existence is somewhat questionable. If Human Resource professionals base their entire development centres on identifying attitudes and personality traits, the foundations might be rather shaky. Even if they do exist, there is little chance of them being changed, so, again, their role in a development centre must be questioned.

The Justification for Personality and Attitudes in Development Centres

While there might be a justification for introducing personality and attitudes into development centres, this is not for measuring the development needs of the employees. It is for helping the individual to identify what aspects of their work they like and what aspects they dislike.

Attitude questionnaires can be extremely effective in helping people to find out more about themselves. With this information, they are in a better position to discuss with the Human Resources staff whether they would find a particular new position satisfying or stressful. They can then plot their careers based upon the direction they wish to head. This does not, though, guarantee that they would be effective after undertaking new responsibilities.

Of course, the behaviourists would still deny the existence of attitudes and just refer to the satisfiers and dissatisfiers as generalised rewarded or punished conditions.

The Formats that Development Centres can Take

The format for the development centre is a direct consequence of the philosophical base that the Human Resource function adopts. Needless to say, adamant protagonists of one particular philosophy would claim that the people who operate centres based on a different philosophy are wasting their time.

The Personality Format

If the focus of the philosophy is on personalities, the emphasis of the centre will be on proven, validated personality questionnaires that will help the candidates to understand themselves and help the assessors to understand the candidates. There will also be a great deal of time spent on interviews.

Enormous research has been conducted into systems such as the Myers Briggs Type Indicator (MBTI) to correlate personalities with occupational successes and with input competences. Approximate personality profiles can be drawn up for the desired job holder and the candidate's actual profile compared with that. Whilst not conclusive, the results of the MBTI will help shape the subsequent interviews. The closeness of the match between desired and actual input competences can then be discussed.

Whilst some organizations will rely heavily on research by psychological consultancies, others might want to draw up their own profiles of desired personalities. This risks only current good performers being used to produce the desired personality profiles and the possibility of cloning taking place. Developing clones of previous job holders might be appropriate in a static business world, but in the dynamic state of most companies, cloning just freezes the staff in a bygone age.

If the match is close, the candidate can probably be developed, as the raw material and propensity for development will be present. If the fit is not close enough, it will not be worth the time or money trying to develop the staff and, even if they were developed, they would probably be unhappy in the new role.

The Attitude Format

With the emphasis on attitudes, a range of questionnaires and surveys will be used to highlight the values and the preferred styles of operation for the candidates. Again the actual attitudes can be compared with the profile of desired attitudes.

In addition to the self report questionnaires, immediate contacts of the individual might be asked to complete surveys. Receiving information from managers, subordinates, peers and even customers and suppliers has become popular in the form of 360^0 feedback. In estimating the attitudes of another person, no one is neutral. We all have our own attitudes which we probably consider to be pretty good. Assessment of other people is, therefore, usually by comparison with ourselves. The advantage of 360^0 feedback is that the biases of one person should be evened out by the biases of someone else.

Apart from using questionnaires, the candidates' attitudes might be assessed by putting them into a range of different situations that are new to them. These situations might be in the form of group exercises or role-plays. Because they have no prior experience of the tasks, they are likely to 'revert to type' and act according to their attitudes rather than behave in a way that has previously been learnt.

Objective recording of the various behaviours shown across all the tasks should enable the underlying attitudes that caused the behaviours to be identified. These attitudes can be compared with the results of the different questionnaires and consistencies and inconsistencies can be noted. Any inconsistencies would be followed up by interviews.

Drawing up the attitude profiles of the desired job holder also remains a problem, as the same dangers of cloning can occur as with personality. Additionally, it is difficult for the Human Resources advisers to include a desired attitude that they may personally find offensive or that contravenes their own personal attitude-code of what is right and what is wrong.

The Behavioural Format

The behaviourists will be looking for objective and specific evidence of the candidate's output competences and their actual knowledge, skills and judgements, so that these can be subtracted from the desired requirements for the next job. They will also be looking for anything that indicates that the applicant is likely to be able to learn the new components.

The emphasis of the centre will be on past achievements and observable evidence of abilities in exercises and role-plays that are as close to the reality of the next job as possible; there will also be less time spent on interviews. This is quite different from the attitude approach. The parts regarding past achievements, which will be admitted as evidence, will occur where the same output competences are required in the new job that are present in the candidate's current job.

Additionally, it is possible that the new job requires a competence which the candidate does not currently have. However, if the candidate can demonstrate an output competence which comprises similar knowledge, skills and judgements to the competence required in the new job, it is likely that the candidate will be able to learn the new competence.

The Sources of Feedback

The sources of feedback will be determined largely by the format of the development centre and how this balances in relation to personality, attitudes and behaviour.

For Personality Formats

The personality format uses most of the feedback from the results of the personality tests, as well as the comparison between these findings and the research conducted by the originators of the test. The development equation of:

desired personality – actual personality = non-development needs
  for the next job   of the candidate   + development needs

still holds, but most of the gap between the desired and the actual will be, by definition of personalities, non-development. The non-development solutions might include career changes, or even company changes.

The other major source of the feedback will be from the various interviews that would have been held.

The Attitude Format

For the attitude approach, the feedback will come from the attitude surveys and styles questionnaires that have been completed by the candidates themselves, and by others who know them well, in the form of 360^0 feedback.

Additionally, there will be feedback available from the collation of the observations of participants in the role-plays and exercises. These exercises, though, will be ones where the candidates have no prior experience – so their underlying attitudes rather than their learnt responses can be seen. Some of the problems of using these forms of exercise – which are too remote from real life – are noted in Chapter 7.

The interpretation of the attitude is made by the trained observers, who compare their observations and agree upon the underpinning reason or explanation for the behaviours that they have seen. This explanation is what they would term the *attitude*. It is clearly important to see clusters of behaviours, rather than just relying upon one. Anybody interested in body language will confirm the folly of always interpreting folded arms as meaning aggression: it could mean that the person is cold, or that they have spilled lunch down their front and are trying to hide the evidence.

It is only by groupings of behaviours that we can be more confident of an underlying attitude. Regard should be made, however, to cultural differences as the body language exhibited by people from one culture could have quite different meanings if used by people from other races. Indeed some development centres have fallen foul of racial discrimination legislation because they have not given sufficient thought to the various interpretations of the same behaviour that can be made.

The Behavioural Format

This is the approach which generates the greatest amount of objective material for feedback. Analysis of past performance and previous reports and appraisals will show behaviours and output competences from the past. Observations in exercises, discussions and role-plays, that are very close to the work that the individuals would be doing in the next job, would provide evidence of current output competences and levels of knowledge, skills and judgements. Once these have been listed for the desired next job, the process of measuring the development centre candidates against the same criteria becomes straightforward.

How the Feedback might be Handled

The 'Feedback Formula', outlined in Chapter 4, suggests that we should:

1. Let the person see what they have done.
2. Let them see the effect of their behaviour.
3. Agree a change.

The Personality Format

The Feedback Formula presents some major difficulties for the personality format. Firstly, because personalities are internal to the individual we cannot show anything observable. Secondly we cannot let the candidates see the effects of their personality, only the effects of their behaviour. Thirdly, and most importantly, we cannot agree a change as they cannot change their personality. We, therefore, either have to give up using the Feedback Formula with all the reasons and benefits covered in Chapter 4 or we have to fit the information we have into the formula.

If we do not use the formula, the feedback will fail on most of the 'Ten Rules for Giving Feedback' (see Chapter 4); it will be subjective, non-specific and inactionable, with the trainer saying, in essence, 'Your personality does not fit'. For example:

> The next job demands a personality with high sociability and medium dominance – which you don't have!

To comply with the Feedback Formula, we can let the candidate see what they have done by showing them the results of the personality instruments we have used. To let them see the effects of those results, we can show comparisons of research which produced the desired personality profile, but we cannot objectively claim that their personality will always, and predictably, guarantee certain output competences. Again we cannot agree a change to their personality.

The formula and the material produced can be used effectively on the non-development needs and the career guidance. We can show the applicants the results of their personality questionnaires, we can explain the profile for the desired job and let them see the effects of a mismatch of personality traits. This evidence could come from research in the area by the instrument suppliers. We can then agree, or at least discuss, with the staff where their aspirations might best be channelled, so that they gain what they are seeking from their careers.

The Attitude Format

The same problems of applying the Feedback Formula to personality arise when they are applied to attitudes. The very nature of attitudes being internal to the individual prevent the first stage of 'letting them see what they did'. Feedback based upon attitudes will be just as subjective and non-specific, though it might be actionable if the attitude is not held very strongly.

We can come close to the first stage of the Formula if we can show all the behavioural evidence which led us to conclude a certain attitude underpinned it. If the applicant agrees with our interpretation we can move on to the second stage and let them see the effects of that attitude. We are still on fairly shaky ground, though, unless we can supply so many examples to support our assumptions. Now we have another danger. If the recipient is a 'wine glass', they can only take about three items of criticism before their glass fills up and they move into Divisions 1, 2 or even 3 (See Chapter 5: How People Receive Feedback). Alternatively, habituation might set in and cause their attention to wane and lose track of an argument. For example:

> The next job requires a person who believes in the importance of genuine consultation with people in a meeting to gain their views. Your attitude seems to be that you should make your decision in advance and then sell that to the meeting.

Clearly this type of feedback is more open to argument.

The Behavioural Format

Here the Feedback Formula can be applied perfectly. The direct objective evidence, taken both from past employment records and from observation during the development centre, provides the material for the first stage of 'what they did' and the second stage of 'the effect'. The third stage, to 'agree a change', is easy to communicate as it will be in the form of output competences broken down into knowledge, skills and judgements. It is then easy to set up detailed development plans so that the applicant can acquire the new competences. Equally, if the difference between desired and actual output competences is too great to spend the time and the money, this can also be explained in a way that confronts the behaviours, and not the personality and attitudes, which might be so close to the individual. For example:

> The next job requires a person who has the competence to conduct consultative meetings with representatives from client organizations.

In the exercise meeting that you led, you used a directive style that communicated what you wanted to achieve. This had the effect of influencing the views of the other participants at the meeting. You will need to develop the output competence of consulting other people in a meeting for their views.

In this example the detailed breakdown into knowledge, skills and judgements might show that the actual gap is relatively small and could be filled with appropriate coaching and delegation.

Review

The distinction between input and output competences, and between personality, attitudes and behaviours, is crucial before a decision can be made on the purpose of development centres, how they are to be designed and what form of feedback the candidates at the centre are to receive.

CHECKLIST FOR THE TRAINER

- What is your stance on input v output competences?
- What is the purpose of your development centres?
- Should your development centres focus more on personality, attitudes or behaviours?
- What form will your feedback to candidates take?

Summary

Feedback is probably the most important of all trainer skills. If trainees cannot be helped to see what they are doing right, they may not be able to repeat it. If they are not helped to change what they are doing wrong they will never improve. Ironically, feedback is also probably the most complicated trainer skill.

Instructors must be able to distinguish feedback, where there is a right and a wrong answer, from debriefing, where there is not. They must be able to give feedback and receive it themselves. They must be able to identify when their learners have received enough criticism and not only know what to do, but be able to do it. The contexts of feedback and debrief cover all the areas of training and development from one-to-one to group training and the climate the trainers set for their training needs careful planning.

The use and abuse of observers and video are crucial for trainers to understand, as is their selection of the correct training technique for each type of learning.

Debriefing training sessions is another vital instructor skill and involves not only handling the interactions of the participants but preventing them slipping back into feedback. Organizing observers, syndicates and reporters must all be considered so that nothing is left to chance.

Trainers must decide whether their feedback remains within the confines of the training environment or extends to reports being sent back to managers.

Finally, as the role of training specialists spreads into other aspects of Human Resources Development, trainers are increasingly involved in designing and running development centres to audit the competence of the organization and to match succession planning with people's career ambitions. This is the ultimate form of feedback as the content of the message might affect the rest of a person's life.

Further Reading

Burnard, P (1992) *Counselling Skills Training: A sourcebook of activities for trainers*, Kogan Page, London.

Fletcher, S (1992) *Competence-Based Assessment Techniques*, Kogan Page, London.

Honey, P and Mumford, A (1983) *The Manual of Learning Styles*, self-published, Maidenhead.

Leigh, D (1991) *a Practical Approach to Group Training*, Kogan Page, London.

McCallum, C (1992) *How to Design and Introduce an Appraisal Training System*, Kogan Page, London.

Mager, R (1991) 'The Mager Library', Kogan Page, London:

— (with Peter Pipe) *Analysing Performance Problems*, second edn

— *Developing Attitude Toward Learning*, second edn

— *Goal Analysis*, second edn

— *Making Instruction Work*

— *Measuring Instructional Results*, second edn

— *Preparing Instructional Objectives*, second edn.

Moon, P (1993) *Appraising Your Staff*, Kogan Page, London

Moreno, J L (1953) *Who Shall Survive? Foundations of sociometry, group psychotherapy and sociodrama*, Beacon House, New York.

Parsloe, E (1992) *Coaching, Mentoring and Assessing: A practical guide to developing competence*, Kogan Page, London.

Scott, C D and Jaffe, D T (1992) *Empowerment: Building a committed workforce*, Kogan Page, London.

Shea, G F (1992) *Mentoring: A guide to the basics*, Kogan Page, London.

Skinner, B F (1953) *Science and Human Behaviour*, Macmillan, New York.

Spinks, T and Clements, P (1993) *A Practical Guide to Facilitation Skills: A real world approach*, Kogan Page, London.